# A Taste of Hope

# A Taste of Hope

Mac McKeown

*A Taste of Hope*
Copyright © 2023 Mac McKeown. All rights reserved.

All rights reserved. No part of this publication may be reproduced, distributed, or transmitted in any form or by any means, including photocopying, recording, or other electronic or mechanical methods, without the prior written permission of the publisher, except in the case of brief quotations embodied in critical reviews and certain other noncommercial uses permitted by copyright law.

ISBN: 979-8-88759-905-2 - paperback
ISBN: 979-8-88759-906-9 - ebook

# DEDICATION

This book is dedicated to my loving wife Marguerite and our three amazing sons; Kevin, Brian, and Shawn. They too have endured their own experiences that are described in the book.

I would like to also dedicate this to all those who have dealt with, or are experiencing a traumatic event in their life. You are not alone as there have been many before you. You've got this! Stay strong and do not be a victim.

# PREFACE

There are always moments in our lives that we feel might make a good human-interest story. An idea that provides people the insight of how to make it through something tough. Perhaps it is a survival manual on herbs, shelters, hunting etc. Something from the real world that's worth writing about. Then there are those who speak or write with words so eloquent they transport the reader to a realm of imagination with their brilliant descriptions.

I had always wanted to be a writer, however I wanted it to be profound and with purpose. Time falls away for some of us. We fail to seize that time, thinking that opportunities will always be present before us. A terrible thought process that has robbed me from so many opportunities.

As you read through these chapters you will come upon my first life obstacle of fighting an illness on behalf of our firstborn son. My wife and I were a complete mess. Yet halfway through the three-year ordeal I felt inspired to write about it. A baseline of arguing between her and I, along with the lack of opportunity for things like a vibrant internet as well as independent publishing companies.

Time passed and life became filled with parental duties and work, with desire and inspiration to grow my career. Our passion for life was always strong and wavered only when our spirits were at the bottom of what we thought we could tolerate. Writing a book was only a glimmer of a thought at best. Life was consuming me.

When each life challenge occurred the idea always came shortly after. Write a book. Well, it was all dismissed as we were in our mid 50's and we wanted to enjoy life in our new home in Florida. Warm all the time with plenty of things to do. A book? No thanks, that was a fleeting idea that I once had. I am no novelist who can inspire the world with an ideology or an incredible story that takes them to far away galaxies or medieval battles.

Then came my wife's diagnosis of Frontotemporal Dementia and my world was dissolving like a snowman at the gates of hell. My experiences have now been so accumulative that through my self-reflection my awareness of success in life was not accomplished without thinking, WOW, look what I have been through. I could not capture all of my challenges, but I wanted to highlight the big ones. The challenges that threatened the lives of family.

This book is to demonstrate to people that tragedy can be overcome. A challenge can be met with love and compassion. Determination with perseverance is a foundation of success. Don't think you have it? Don't be a victim and say you can't do it. I know it feels that way at first. Pull up your big girl or big boy pants and push through. Even if you have to act brave and cry in private, we all have the determined beast within our hearts to make it through those challenges without terrible self-inflicted outcomes like drug abuse, alcoholism, running away from your life and loved ones. They do not solve the problem. Your heart, mind and soul solve them.

Please enjoy reading this. Place yourself in the story and imagine the complexity of the dynamics. Take it all in and wonder from time to time what you would have done. There are messages to hear, and eventually recommendations to help, but they are not the solutions for everyone.

The only thing someone with insight will get out of the intent of this book is the unwritten words of the story. Those words are the conclusion that I hope inspire most:

This family went through a lot, they stayed together, he honored his wife like most should, but some don't. They are a good example of how to survive life's challenges of mortality.

There are people in the book that I do not name. If they participated in negative aspects of our lives, I kept their names out for their own protection. Situations occur, and we should move on from events that have haunted us. I however have a difficult time letting things go. I forgive, but I don't forget. When actions become repetitious in life, then a different assessment should be considered. I have experienced a lot of bullying in my life, in various forms. Therefore, the disclosure of events here in the following chapters are some experiences of bullying too. Yes, adults subconsciously bully people face to face. Perhaps I have as well. I may not have been aware, but I am truly sorry.

If you have actively participated in events of my life and I failed to mention you or that event, I am truly sorry. My goal was to capture the umbrella description of 36 + years, and not to rewrite a diary. My gratitude for those who have been such a pillar of love and friendship in our lives know who you are. You are all blessed human beings who have hearts of divinity.

I was listening to a podcast interview with Andre De Shields who is an American actor, singer, dancer, director, and choreographer. Upon receiving his first Tony award at age 73 his acceptance speech struck my forehead like a two by four piece of oak. Three rules he stated were, "1: surround yourself with people whose eyes light up when they see you coming. 2. Slowly is the fastest way to get to where you want to be. 3: The top of one mountain is the bottom of the next, so keep climbing." At 60 years old, I discard those relationships that are most taxing. Those that make my stomach uneasy when I see them. I want happiness and friendships that enjoy life. I have 25 years left on this planet if I am lucky. May it be in peace to enjoy my family, events, and joy of living life.

CHAPTER

1

# PURSUIT OF DREAMS

I had a unique outlook that probably fit with a percentage of young men in my generation. I wanted a good job, a family, and kids as soon as possible. My mother was 42 when she had me. I wanted to be able to be there as a dad and enjoy my empty nest at a decent age. Grandkids early enough so I can play with and enjoy them as well. Graduating from High School in 1981 in a small town in Maine, I had little direction on where I wanted to go in life. Didn't have a solid college plan. Applied to Maine Maritime Academy to become a Merchant Marine and was not accepted due to missing information. A transcript of my SATs were sent to me, not the college. They requested I reapply the following year. There was a shipyard in the town I graduated from, alongside a river that leads to the Atlantic Ocean some 13 miles downriver. It was there that I took a job working 3$^{rd}$ shift. I was a laborer, and later a spray painter.

Actually, I was doing very well as a 19-year-old. Bought a mobile home, had a Chevy Camaro, which my father helped with by trading in his Chevy Impala. Made friends at the shipyard and was enjoying the bachelor life. However, the internal voice inside of me began calling out. Find someone special to spend the rest of your life with and start a family.

A popular three-wheeler hit the streets, which a group of us from the shipyard would transport to sand pits and spend time there for an afternoon. I had a pet Boa constrictor and a cat. They got along great if I kept a barrier of glass between them. Dating, dancing, movies, and night clubbing was a routine thing. But it was not what I wanted. I dated someone for a little over a year, but it didn't work out. She went to college, and we simply went different ways.

I finally decided to join a dating service. This was of course before the computer era. Filling out a 12-page questionnaire about myself was daunting. I would receive a mailed name with a location and phone number. It was my option to call or request another name. I tried two different dates that were not even close to a match with my personality regarding likes and dislikes. By request, another name came to me. Marguerite. She was from 3 towns away to the west. I called and we spoke for a little bit. Then we talked again in a day or two. She graduated the same year as I did. Side note: She is only 33 days older than I am. Both of us were 24 years old at the time. Got a lot of teasing on both sides that she was a cradle robber and that I was chasing cougars. Anyway, we decided to take a chance and meet that Friday. It happened to be February 14th, 1986. We met at an agreed location and went out to dinner. I didn't care where we were, I simply enjoyed talking to her.

We spent that evening talking. In fact, we didn't say goodnight until close to 2 a.m. I drove home after dropping her off with excitement, hoping she felt the same connection. I couldn't wait to talk to her again. We did. We couldn't get enough of each other. The connections we had in so many topics, it finally was evident that the dating service earned their fee, which I began to doubt.

How do you know that the person of your dreams, the woman that would be a best friend and partner as well as a great mother to your children is in front of you? It all comes together in what I refer to as a *Taste of Hope*. Sure, it sounds quirky, but you will see throughout this book that the *Taste of Hope* has many flavors. This flavor was one of strawberries and cream. She was soothing, kind, like no one I had ever met. She possessed a degree of innocence and wholesomeness which I had not seen in anyone for a long time. Marguerite's shining light frequently reminded me of Karen Carpenter. Not because of her voice, or that she resembled her. She was the kind of woman I'd imagined being with since my first boyhood crush listening to Carpenter's voice on the radio. It was soothing and gentle, stable and confident to my ears. Marguerite was all that to me and more.

So, 63 days later, or 2 months and 4 days, I proposed to her. Knowing that I had found my soulmate. The woman that I would trust with my heart and the divine nurturing of our future children. We both wanted children and felt as though we had an obligation to raise them in the best way we knew how. Provide safety, love, opportunities, education, foster their interests and talents. We didn't have all the answers, but we knew that love was the best foundation for any child.

3

She said yes, and it was set in our hearts. The question was when, and the opportunity for me was in the fall. I loved autumn however she really didn't want to push it that soon. I then realized that she needed to spend time being excited and planning along with me about our future. Well, we met on a Friday in February. The 14$^{th}$ if you recall. Her idea was to marry the following year which fell on a Saturday the 14$^{th}$ of February. A Catholic wedding, since we were both Catholic. She was more of a practicing Catholic than I. Mid-winter weddings in Maine? How bad could it be? We could retreat to a Caribbean getaway and enjoy some comfortable weather before returning to some of New England's coldest of temperatures.

We married on Valentine's Day in 1987. I was told by a classmate who was later a co-worker at the shipyard that this wedding was incredible. It was as close to a royal wedding as he had ever seen. As for Marguerite and I, we couldn't see the forest for the trees, but we did have an amazing wedding as well as a reception. We were as thrilled as any new couple. Our lives were starting, and the future was wide open.

We did not go to Jamaica, or any other Caribbean Island. Quebec City in Quebec Canada was our destination. They have a winter carnival every year and the 14$^{th}$ or 15 is typically their last day of a weeklong celebration. We froze, to say the least. Walked several blocks to a restaurant in -14 degrees below zero Fahrenheit. That converts to -25 C for those of you who are more familiar with the metric system. A fantastic week we had but decided to cut it short and return home. We had to start our lives as soon as possible. Vacationing is nice, but we had dreams to chase.

We moved into my mobile home that I purchased 5 years previously. This may be thought of as a romantic "B" movie plot. A typical mill / shipyard guy meets a girl, lives in a trailer park, and lives paycheck to paycheck for years as their kids become the local town's troubled youths and have been voted Most Likely Not to Succeed by their school, if they even stayed in school. Honestly only one thing was true. We lived paycheck to paycheck. I worked as much overtime as I could, and we dreamed big. It wasn't before long that the gravity of her hometown called her back, and we decided to move there.

We took up residence on the 2$^{nd}$ floor in an apartment house that her mother owned. Marguerite's grandmother had lived upstairs with Marguerite through most of her teen years. While we were in our mobile home her grandmother passed away. It was there where we chose to go and save our pennies for a down payment on a house.

Marguerite and I were anxious to start a family. However, excitement is sometimes overshadowed by a sudden change in a lifestyle. We were obviously on a fast track for about a year and a half. In today's world we simply *Google* a question and a search engine provides some of the most recent responses. Stress and pregnancy success is easily validated through a host of studies from colleges, hospitals, and researchers. This was not so easy in 1987.

Moving into her familiar environment and hometown gave way to a more relaxed and settled partner. It was after a long day of work that I returned home to have her waiting for me at the door. "Hi Sweetie, or should I say Hi future dad." My eyes shot directly to her face. Was she toying with me or was she making me the happiest guy she'd ever met? Yes! She confirmed it with that lovely smile, and we held one another out of sheer joy and excitement.

In the words of Matthew McConaughey, "Well All right, all right, all right!" We were on our way and my dream was taking place every waking moment. Now for those of you who are already parents let me say, we did the traditional things that a first parent does. Those of you who are not parents yet, well, I am not going to spoil it for you. Find out for yourself because there is no wrong way or right way as long as safety for mom and baby are considered. Eleven days after her due date, during a full moon, her water broke. Why not? The moon moves oceans, it was about time it moved this baby!! So, we went to the hospital and within one hour of labor his heart rate dropped below 80 bpm. Well, there is obviously something going on with the umbilical cord, said the doctor. We are going to have to prepare for surgery and do a "C" section.

Happy ending – our son was born with all his fingers and toes, screaming with all the resistance he could muster as though he was trying to say "Just give me eleven more days….. Please!!" But we were happy as could be. After all, a newborn has a quality all its own. It is the purest event of humanity's existence. This *Taste of HOPE* has dreams deeply embedded in every touch, good night kiss, diaper change, and spit up, a unique thing that I believe that we all experience. Yes the *Taste of HOPE* was of sweet floral scents combined with fresh air, sunshine, and all the attributes that put a spring in your step and draw you home like the gravity of a black hole. I couldn't wait to get back from work every day.

We yearn for that small little human being to hopefully enjoy the life that they were given without choice. Experience all the wonders of what this third rock from the sun offers. What can we do to provide that enrichment? Will they be a contributor to mankind? To me the *Taste of HOPE* has many parallels with the <u>fresh</u> scent of a newborn. That lovely smell that a baby possesses after a bath and perhaps a little baby powder. However, the baby powder doesn't make the glorious aroma so much as the newness of human life in its first few months. Perhaps one of my most favorite yet rarely enjoyed pleasures in life.

Nine months of preparing mentally for parenthood and now it's here. His first name we chose almost without thinking–Kevin. It felt right and we were as blessed as we were excited. Focus has now shifted. That child gets all the attention from both of us. Breaks are provided, outings are made and the care that goes into every aspect of this boy's day is to say the least, daunting. However, the joy of watching this miniature human being grow and develop with his own special actions or gestures is so rewarding. Every parent out there has a photo or a story of what some of their favorite moments were. Honestly with today's cell phone and video capabilities it is a wonder that their whole day isn't documented to some extent.

We took a trip to Boston one spring Saturday morning. The goal for the day was Quincy Market. The three of us visited the infamous Quincy Market, and also took in a lot of the sites of surrounding buildings. I recall walking by the infamous Faneuil Hall as I pushed the stroller while Marguerite was to my left side and the hall was on my right. There was a young man, perhaps close to my age, who was wearing a dark gray dingy hooded sweatshirt pulled over his head. It was oversized as it shrouded his face like a jedi hooded cloak in a Star Wars episode. As I neared him and was parallel to where he sat, he lifted up his head, pointed a finger in my direction and said, "Take care of that boy, you hear me?" I was startled as he singled me out amongst the crowd of visitors, tourists, and Bostonians. "You can count on it" I replied as though I owed him an answer. We walked about 50 to 75 feet beyond that, and I stopped. I turned slightly to *tie my shoe,* but it wasn't untied. I wanted to watch the young man to see if he was commenting to any other passersby commuters, but he wasn't. He sat slumped over but as we were about to continue on, he stood up with his head still down, and disappeared into the crowd.

It wasn't a message from a burning bush, or a vision in a dream yet this guy gave me the heebie jeebies. To this day I do not know the nature of his comment. I am not saying he was an angel that appeared to give me a warning about the future or anything like that. All I am saying is that is the only time in my 60 years that anyone has done anything like that. The future events of later years made me ponder his comment with a depth of wonder.

Eight months go by in a flash. Kevin is walking, and first words are being spoken. Wow, what an exciting time. Then she utters the unexpected words. "Honey I am pregnant". Exciting yes, overwhelming, far more than the excitement. The questions come flooding in from her and family all with variations of excitement and criticism.

# A Taste of Hope

I remember having discussions with her about strategies with money and diapers, which room he'd have and so on. We were not careful with family planning but that didn't matter. We were going to meet the challenge of having two kids 16 months apart in a positive way. Who wouldn't ? What are you going to do? Hey – put that second baby back! No, of course we press forward, and it certainly wasn't the equivalent of having twins or triplets.

The week of Thanksgiving in 1989 we chose a date to have her second "C" section. The doctor said that her uterus was thinned from the previous "C" section. A phrase that they called a "window". So, to lighten the mood I did what an idiot dad would say at the doctor's office. So, does that mean she has a womb with a view? I would have had the same results having been to a New England baked bean supper on a Saturday night and attending church the following morning without being able to control the side effects of the baked beans from the night before. They both made a subtle attempt to pretend that I was not in the room. Well, it's not going to be an easy car ride home after that one, was my thought. She didn't disappoint. I'd embarrassed her, but I was trying to lighten the air knowing that she had to have another surgery.

Our second son Brian was born, and we fell back into the very same euphoria that we experienced with Kevin. That sweet feeling that takes you away from all your worries when you hold a newborn again. That *Taste of Hope*, it never gets old. The sweetest flavor that fills your mental palette with all purity in flavor imaginable. Those moments are never a long stretch of time. The deception of time combined with continuous pulls of parenthood dilute the oxytocin high when you are embellishing the moments of that taste of hope. Life and its never-ending pursuit of problems mixed in with our days.

It makes us not only stronger, but smarter, braver, more determined. It really shapes us as adults. I have met some people that have faced little to no adversity. Envious I was (spoken in Yoda's voice for theatrical effect) but later realized that when the smallest of problems come their way it is like watching a human melt down over something that a survivor of adversity would snicker at and solve over a coffee while driving to work.

"Money isn't everything, as long as you have enough" is a favored quote by Malcom Forbes. We unequivocally didn't have enough. Now the bread winner had to work more. Pick up some overtime at the shipyard. Let's watch our spending while we have disagreements about money and where it is spent, by whom, and when blah blah blah oh my GOD!! What is going on? This treadmill is moving a little too fast and when you look at it, we have only been married for two years. In later years we both admitted to one another that we were terrified because it wasn't what we envisioned. It wasn't part of our pipedream of what it would be like to have a marriage and kids. The stress is high at times, but then we compared notes with the world. We are not being bombed during a wartime or having to practice retreating to fallout shelters. We have grocery stores that have a surplus of food, we are 26 years old and making our way in the world. Let's not squabble over things, and let's enjoy this.

Parents have to be adaptive multi-tasking problem solvers, juggling an ever growing list of schedules and duties. They just have to find their groove, and we were settling into ours. We plateaued and were enjoying all that our lives had before us. Kevin was 2 and Brian was still a toddler. Most of our routine was praying that at 8 months old Brian would sleep through the night for once. We knew that there would come a time where we could settle in as a growing family, with a comfortable and sweet routine.

I was offered to work on a crew in Portland Maine where my company had a dock and a drydock. My crew of coworkers performed a metalizing process of bonding aluminum to steel. The job was time sensitive, and pushed for 12-hour days, 6 a.m. to 6 p.m. beginning in late September and into October of 1990. Portland was an hour away from the town I lived in so travel time as well as prep time made it more like a 15-to-16-hour day. This would run typically 5 to 6 days a week and occasionally a Sunday in the mix if time was sensitive enough to meet a deadline. It was a naval ship contract.

It was during this time that Marguerite began noticing that Kevin wasn't feeling right. He appeared sluggish and slept in during the morning. There were times that he slept in until 8:30 or 9:00 a.m. A blessing at first with Brian not sleeping through the nights as long as he did, but this was different. We knew this 2-year-old should be bouncing off the walls at least at 7 a.m. She took him to the pediatrician and they basically said he was fine. Enjoy the sleep-in schedule as he is growing, and every kid is different. They even compared our personalities with how he was behaving. You and your husband are both calm, quiet people so this may be how he is adapting to the family. He feels calm and is comfortable with his atmosphere.

Then a never ending cold developed that lasted beyond 3 weeks, which they passed off as perhaps allergies. Kevin was still tired all the time–who wasn't? Marguerite was watching the boys alone while I was working 12 hour shifts and it just seemed exhausting to describe our days let alone live them. We bought into it when any legitimate and reasonable explanation was offered to us. But then there was unexplained bruising on Kevin. Some small spots and some of very suspicious sizes mostly on his legs, and some on his torso.

I began to wonder what was going on while I was not home. Suspicion flooded my thinking and I tried to wrap my brain around the possible scenarios that would cause this. It was immediately clear to me that the concern in my wife's eyes and the care in her voice was not from a woman who was afraid of the fallout of child abuse allegations, but that she too didn't know and was very concerned.

"He is a two-year-old that is going to bump into stuff, and playing around in the house or outside will certainly yield a bruise or two" was the pediatrician's diagnosis. He was okay. But 9 to 12 bruises? It doesn't seem right. During the month of October and including the second half of September, Marguerite took Kevin to the doctors approximately 9 times. The receptionist was apparently tired of our frequent visits and she told my wife that she needed to let the cold take its course and to stop calling. He was going to be fine, and she was an overprotective mother.

That was the last straw for me. Let's go somewhere else, I said.

Halloween came around and we dressed Kevin up as a pumpkin. He was so tired that he couldn't walk so we pulled him in the wagon and carried him to a door. Isn't it funny how you can be so immersed in a situation that you really don't see what is actually happening? But then it hit me. A woman who answered the door as I held him in my arms looked at Kevin and said, "He should be dressed as a ghost not a pumpkin, look how pale he is". I was shocked at how right she was. It was then that we turned around and went home. So while I was working another 12-hour day Marguerite found another pediatrician who was willing to take on a new patient and was very curious to see Kevin. The new pediatrician told Marguerite that she needed to go and see a blood specialist in Portland. He told her to call as soon as she got home. He wasn't sure, but he said he thought that his symptoms were urgent, and these specialists could help.

Marguerite called the number when she got home. "Hello – Maine Children's Cancer Program, can I help you?" She explained to me that she hung up immediately. Wait a minute she thought, I must have dialed the wrong number. She looked at the number and slowly dialed it again. The same voice answered the same way "Hello – Maine Childr…." She hung up. Panic paralyzed her. No no no this can't be happening. They gave me the wrong number; I'll call the pediatrician's number back for the correct number. She called the pediatrician to request the correct number. "Well Mrs. McKeown, please read to us the number you have." She read the number slowly and the office receptionist confirmed it was the right number. "We have been in touch with them, and they are expecting your call Mrs. McKeown. Go ahead and call them, you have the right number." Marguerite called and upon the receptionist answering she apologized for hanging up on them the previous two times.

When I arrived home from my long day, I found her sitting on the floor exhausted from crying alone while the two boys played. Holding and consoling her, she was able to tell me the brief yet terrifying story of her day. They believe Kevin has Leukemia. "We have to go see them tomorrow to verify with some sort of test. What are we going to do?" She wept the words with despair and shock.

I couldn't wrap my head around it. Leukemia? I knew what it was only by word association but did not know what the details of the disease was.

I remember muddling through the evening, baths after supper, bedtime stories and finally sleep. Thoughts of denial or requesting that a slammed door would wake me up and realize that it was a Sunday morning. Marguerite would lay there staring at me with her bright smile and warm green eyes. That never happened. It wasn't a dream. Later, around 9 p.m. I was teetering on the edge of exhaustion from a 12-hour day and trying to comprehend this news. She got a babysitter for Brian so that we could go to the appointment with just Kevin.

I recall that I was awakened by her crying, which I felt terrible about. She couldn't sleep, and yet that is all I wanted to do. "How can you sleep?" she demanded to know. "I have to recharge, or I am not going to be enough for anyone, come tomorrow. There is nothing we can do about anything at this moment. He is safe in his room; Brian is safe, and we will deal with this tomorrow. We cannot solve anything tonight." I quickly fell back to sleep. I felt immense guilt but I knew I had to provide for our family what she couldn't, and I'd need my energy.

We drove to our 10 a.m. appointment. There we were at Maine Children's Cancer Program. There was no one in the waiting room. A doctor emerged from behind a door and introduced himself as Dr. Cohen. He said that he understood our confusion and that he was going to perform some tests. "However," he said with a pause, "we believe this is Leukemia."

CHAPTER

## 2

# SOMEONE WAKE ME UP PLEASE!

A nurse appeared and brought us both back into an exam room. I couldn't tell you anything about that room from that November 2$^{nd}$ day in 1990, with the exception of a chair leaning against a wall where Marguerite sat, and another beside it which I sat on, briefly.

"We are going to conduct a test where we look at a sample of Kevin's bone marrow and view it beneath a microscope. We will be able to tell right away what he has." Marguerite and I were both in agreement, though we hadn't even begun to consider the procedure. How were they going to sample his bone marrow? Some kind of device similar to an x-ray?

Now the locomotive of our lives was flying down the track. If I looked in any direction but forwards my world began to blur.

A sense of foreboding washed over me. The world around me was muffled, distant. I fought to focus on the doctor's voice, "First we will numb his tissue to reduce the pain sensation. This is a quick test, and it is over as quickly as it begins. It is far too risky to place children under anesthesia" said the doctor. The nurse looked at me and gestured to the exam table that was in the center of the room, "Sir if we can have Kevin lay face down and perhaps if you can help when it's time, you could hold his hands and arms". Sure, okay I thought. They didn't ask Marguerite to help which seemed odd. I wondered why.

I explained to Kevin that he had to lay down on the table face down and that I wasn't going anywhere. I was going to be right there holding his hand. The nurse gently lifted his shirt upwards towards his chest, unbuttoned his pants and dropped those to his knees before helping Kevin lay face down. They prepared the area with betadine and alcohol, then applied a topical numbing agent to reduce the feeling of the pinch of the Novocaine needle.

A couple of minutes went by and the needle was about to be administered. "Sir, can you hold Kevin's hands and wrists please. This is going to sting a little but it will be quick". My focus was solely on Kevin and wondering what was going on, his thoughts and fears.

First the nurse held Kevin's legs and I his wrist upon recognizing that it was my cue. A surface administration of the Novocain through a shallow puncture, then a little deeper with an administration of more from the syringe, and deeper the needle went until I thought it couldn't go any further. Kevin was crying. He had cried at doctor's visits before, with vaccination shots, but this was far more intense.

As I consoled Kevin and they explained that they were almost done, he had to remain lying down and still. I watched the doctor prepare a second needle at the exam room's prep tray. You may have seen similar things at the dentist or another doctor's office where there is this little adjustable height tray that they use as the staging area for their tools. A minute or so passed by. I never looked at my wife and she never got up from her seat. We were both frozen. I had tunnel vision.. The doctor turned toward the exam table with a syringe that held a needle. It looked more like an 1/8 diameter drill bit without the blades, longer than most needles I had ever seen.

"Okay Mr. McKeown I'm going to need you to hold Kevin's arms really good for me – Do you understand?" I think I muttered a yes, or perhaps shook my head yes. "Kevin, try not to move okay" said the doctor. Then he plunged the needle into the center of where the alcohol and Betadine antiseptic was prepped on his hip. He paused, Kevin screamed, and then came the rest of the needle.. He leaned over Kevin's torso and pushed the second phase in through Kevin's hip bone, where the safest and most abundant source of bone marrow lies. Hearing my son's screams, I could have believed they were cutting off a finger with a hand saw.

"Almost done….. Almost done….. Almost done." Said doctor Cohen. Oh my sweet Jesus what am I doing, I thought. I'm committed to being the keeper of Kevin's arms. I can't let him move. If he bolts in any direction could he break the needle off inside? I've got to keep doing this. Oh God I want to be somewhere else. I'm dreaming, yeah! It's extremely vivid but I am dreaming. Someone please wake me up, I thought, and as I looked at Kevin's face he was beet red. Drool was oozing from his mouth, his eyes were shut tight as though he was splashed with something that made them sting and burn. Then the doctor said the magic words, "All done, you can hold your son."

Marguerite sprung from her seat like a greyhound out of the starting gate. She snatched Kevin up and held him so close, crying with him, reassuring him that mommy was there. The doctor removed the syringe and disappeared from the room while the nurse cleaned up. I couldn't stop pacing the floor, dazed. What the hell just happened? Did that just happen? I felt hot and enclosed like the room was getting smaller. Then I looked at Marguerite and Kevin. He was beginning to settle down. Total fear was all I saw in her face and eyes. Were we now involved in some kind of weird, bizarre medical trial that isn't approved? Who are these people? That was just plain frigging BARBARIC!!

Then I looked at Kevin again and Marguerite spotted it too. He had little red blotches all over his face in a tight pattern from his forehead to his neck. "What is wrong with his face?" Marguerite asked the nurse. "Oh, that is called Petechia." She said like it perfectly normal "What is Petechia"? I asked.

"It is where the tiny blood vessels in his face broke open because of his screaming. He will be fine; it doesn't hurt and it will fade away" she said in a reassuring manner. Oh great – Jesus Mary and Joseph that is just great. This still can't be happening. Neither one of us knew this type of procedure existed. Granted we were young, but it was all incomprehensible. It wasn't fair..

It could have been 20 minutes or an hour before the doctor came back into the room. I could feel my breath shorten and my stomach sink as he asked us both to sit down.

"Sit down, why.... Just say it.... What is it?" Marguerite demanded.

"It's Leukemia" said Doctor Cohen. That was all I heard. My ears stopped working. He continued to talk to Marguerite, explaining the details. She sat there trying to absorb all of this. She was already internalizing this as something wrong she had done. Then there was the guilt that she had from her son screaming so loud that he broke blood vessels in his face. She couldn't prevent that. She internalized her past 2 and ½ years into a narrow funnel of blame and she wasn't going to let another thing happen to her baby.

Me on the other hand, I could not have been more shell shocked and delirious if Mike Tyson hit me once with a left hook and I managed to stay standing. This was no drug-induced effect. I wasn't in my right mind at all. I am grateful that I wasn't driving or doing something dangerous. I had time to try to get it together. I really have never been a Johnny-on-the-Spot kind of person. I needed some time to digest this.

"Mac, you need to call your parents. Ummm excuse me", she said to the nurse "is there a phone we could use, we need to inform our families as soon as possible. We have another son who is with my mom, and Mac needs to call his parents."

Who, what… what are we doing?

"Weren't you listening to the doctor? You need to call your parents, and I am calling my mom to see if she can watch Brian overnight"

"Overnight – why"? It was then that the doctor returned – perhaps because we were demonstrating signs of falling apart right before their eyes and they had to intervene.

"Folks" said the doctor, "make your phone calls, and why don't you go out and take a break for lunch"

"Oh – okay" I responded. "Then we come back here?" I asked like I was confirming something that was already said.

"No, you are going to the 3rd floor of Maine Medical Center, it's the children's wing. They know you are coming so they will be expecting you," confirmed doctor Cohen

"Oh okay, so then we can go home after that appointment?" I inquired.

"No they will handle your details of admitting Kevin," he clarified.

I went back down the rabbit hole of being stunned. Admitting? I called my parents and with a shocked and stunned voice I told my mother that it was confirmed Kevin was diagnosed with Leukemia. We are going to lunch and after that apparently, we are being admitted into Maine Medical Center. I was still fuzzy about what was going on. Information was pouring into my ears and bouncing right back out. My brain didn't want to take on any new information. Marguerite called her mother and cried over the phone.

Wow, she is crying – I'm not crying – should I be crying? I don't feel anything. Is this normal for someone not to break down and lose it? After all, we are talking about our first born. The proverbial front man for parents' dreams and aspirations, yet I am not crying. Oh I am definitely not right because I don't feel anything but numb.

We drove to a local McDonalds, not knowing how long this day from hell was going to last. We both ordered something but neither of us were hungry. We got Kevin a Happy Meal. What a joke. I watched the other little kids running around, while Kevin didn't have the energy to walk from the car to the entrance. What would happen to him, to us, to our lives as a couple? What did we do to make this happen, if there was anything at all? Yet we both took the blame on ourselves.

We had tried to give him the proper nutrition. She breast fed him for months because it was supposed to strengthen his immunity. A routine schedule of naps and proper sleep. Warm clothes, hat and mittens during the cold Maine winter. When Kevin was done eating his happy meal we gathered up the remainder of our unfinished food and headed for the car.

We drove to Maine Medical Center as all of the three locations were within a few miles of one another. If you are from Maine or have been there vacationing, you know that it is difficult for most anything to be within a couple miles of something else. Distance in Maine is typically measured by time, not by mileage. How far away is your hometown from Portland for example? "Oh, I'd say it's a good 40 to 45-minute drive, depending on rush hour, or if flatlanders were in." This could only mean that tourists were in Maine and they are terrible commuters.

We went inside and the lady at the front desk of reception and information. "Can I help you?" she offered

"Yes, we just left the Maine Children's Cancer Program and…."

"This must be Kevin," she smiled looking over the counter. They were expecting us.

We went where she told us and when the elevator doors opened on Kevin's floor, I felt my stomach drop. We walked a little bit more and Kevin wanted to be picked up and carried. He was exhausted and couldn't make it all the way down the hall to the nurse's station.

"You must be the McKeown's," said a nurse from behind the busy station. "And this is Kevin?" she said in the friendliest of voices. "Let's get you to Kevin's room where you can settle in." At this point it was about 1:30 or so and I watched the clock with total wonder. Is that clock on a battery? There has got to be someone from Maintenance that can put a new battery in that clock, it's not moving. You see I learned over the years that fear has a way of slowing down time. Time drags unless you are having a good time. Not fair in the very least, but we will discuss later in this book about what to do with the good moments to make them last.

So, there we were on November 2$^{nd}$, 1990. One day after the referral from the second opinion, two days after Halloween when we wondered what was wrong with our son.

We did a lot of waiting. That evening it was determined that an IV should be started. They brought Kevin to a treatment room. Thankfully they vowed, no needles ever in that room. That room was a sanctuary from having "Ouchy's" as we learned was the term on the 3$^{rd}$ floor for needle sticks. Maine Medical Center is a teaching hospital. Students have to go somewhere to learn and "practice medicine" and the young intern who wanted to get into oncology was going to start the IV on Kevin. Problem is, with a 2 year old with Leukemia it was extremely difficult to find a vein and Mr. Kevin had his fill of needle sticks for the day. The young intern attempted with one of the smallest needles available. He jabbed and missed, jabbed and missed. This went on for several minutes. Kevin was dehydrated from crying. That is when the mother's fury was released. Marguerite burst through the treatment room door and yelled "STOP ! STOP HURTING MY SON!"

"Ma'am we have to start an IV on Kevin," said the intern who was afraid, frustrated and feeling terrible that he was causing this kind of pain to a 2-year-old.

"THEN GET A REAL DOCTOR IN HERE SO IT CAN BE DONE RIGHT"!! She rushed to the table and picked Kevin up and held him close. The room fell silent, and the young intern stepped out into the hallway and wept openly.

Well, I'm not telling her she is wrong. This is a mother whose day has been crushed under a tidal wave of emotions. A woman who had to sit and watch a bone marrow sample being drawn from her first born's hip. She was on the brink of collapse.

She carried him back to the room and rocked him in the rocking chair. It was a valiant retreat and I supported her by silently following. No apologies were uttered. We were simply afraid. A few minutes passed and a nurse came into the room with Marguerite's permission.

She stood silently and Marguerite openly wept while she spoke, "They were hurting my baby, he has been through enough today" she continued sobbing.

"We have a specialist coming up to start the IV. Very skilled and it will be done. Since this is Friday and you have had a long day, we won't do the central line until tomorrow, but we do need to start an IV. Can we try again with someone else? Are you okay with that Mrs. McKeown?" Marguerite conceded and prepped Kevin for the new procedure. She requested to hold him while the IV was started to keep him calm. It was done as quick as a sneeze.

"All done Kevin !" said the phlebotomist. Kevin looked down with red swollen eyes at his hand with the last piece of tape being placed on it and could not hold back the smile and spontaneous laughter all out of relief. I thanked the phlebotomist and the staff of people that were there wanting to do the right thing for the three of us. Marguerite held him in a way that clearly meant no one was going near him for the rest of the night. If there was a taste of hope present, it had no flavor at all. Tasteless yet satisfying with the results that he was given a break.

The following day Kevin was scheduled for surgery. A central line was going to be implanted in a major vein in his chest. A white tube would exit his chest with a bandage guarding it, as well as a large clear approximate 4 x 5-inch adhesive to safeguard it from being accidentally snagged and pulled out.

That afternoon we were visited by Dr. Blattner who was the founder of Maine Children's program and a top-notch child oncologist. Actually, the three doctors were all top-notch oncologists. Dr. Blattner brought us into a conference room down the hall.

"Okay first let me explain my expectations – Don't challenge the staff here like that again. Hurting Kevin was not their intention, and this is a learning hospital, understand?"

Marguerite spoke with clear conviction. "We have been through hell today and they were hurting my son..." her voice cracked and she became emotional once again with sorrow and apologies but she only wanted the best for him and not to be a guinea pig.

We agreed and he explained to us what type of Leukemia Kevin had. Acute Lymphoblastic Leukemia. He told us that if there was ever a "good" strain to have, then he had itt. There are many other strains that are very very difficult. There was nothing we did as parents, it is not genetic, nor do they know the cause. He went on to explain that they work with Boston and Paris, France to compare notes, successes and failures on a regular basis to ensure that the right therapy is working. Then the bomb was dropped.

"Kevin is going to have to stay here for a month. We are going to bombard his body with Chemotherapy, which is all made from plants. It kills cancer cells but it also kills good cells. It will make him sicker, but we have to get him into remission. This means when we look at his bone marrow we cannot detect any Leukemia cells. That doesn't mean that there are none, it simply means that we have decreased the amount drastically. Then he will remain on a regimen of Chemo for the next 2 years."

Marguerite and I held one another's hands and we sat silently. The doctor continued explaining the protocol and also told us the cold hard reality, words that I have never forgotten.

"Your lives will never be the same." But what about after 2 years? Life should go back to normal by then…. Won't it? I couldn't comprehend that message, but I was far too afraid to ask. I think Marguerite was in the same boat because we were both equally silent. He continued telling us that Leukemia is a white blood cancer. It is simply one cell that stops growing to its mature state and divides and multiples. Before long it has so many that even just bumping into furniture can cause bruising from internal bleeding. The platelets that clog bleeds are too few because those malformed white cells are taking over. This was detected back in the 1700's and was known as the white blood disease back then.

Incredibly we were also given the option not to treat Kevin if that is something we chose to do. We didn't have to if it was against our beliefs. We could simply take him home and make him comfortable. I looked at him, puzzled, as though my face could convey my thoughts of "What the hell? No! Who would do such a thing?" He said it was something that he had to put on the table. How does that differ from Euthanasia? We haven't even tried yet. We both said no right away, with unquestionable conviction.

Marguerite and I listened for more of his speech. His voice was heard, but both of us admitted to one another that we lost what he was saying after the whole 1700s history lesson. Each of us began wondering what was in store for us as parents, and individuals. Thoughts flooded each of our minds. She wondered if I was going to leave her, and I wondered the same. We worried about our son Brian and we didn't have the slightest clue of how we were going to survive a month in the hospital. Then he said: "Well I think I have said enough, and there is a lot for each of you to digest by the glazed look in both of your eyes. Go back to your son. Think things over – write down questions and we will see one another on Monday."

"I have one question for you doc. Left untreated with your option that we refused, how long before he expires?" I asked.

"Hmmm, knowing his blood count, I'd have to say a month, maybe two at best. You've made the right choice, trust me. It won't be easy, but it is the right choice," he replied with confidence.

What we didn't anticipate in our journey was that he was 1000 % correct. Yes, I added another zero intentionally. Our lives were going to change, and it wouldn't be due to just the medical treatment. No, no. It is how the world treated us. Work, neighbors, friends, relatives. Sometimes the kindest gestures were from total strangers while others carved deep caverns in our hearts. Our experiences are lessons for you, the reader, to hear, understand and learn from. This disease and those others that we faced over the past 30 years are a lesson for humanity. A positive lesson through bad experiences. You have the ability to offer a positive sweet and mellow taste of hope in someone's life. Know this, if you turn your back in an act of malice, the harm you create is damage done to the heart and mind which is everlasting.

Please join me in the next chapter where I share with you some of the crazy circumstances we were faced with. Heroes and traitors. But please understand this very important element of this book. I am only acknowledging the Heroes by name. Those who have done us wrong will not receive recognition. I am not out to ruin anyone. I simply want to share my story for you the reader to learn and perhaps be the vehicle of change. Collectively my dream with this book is to inspire people to do something that is beyond their comfort level and help someone whose life is riding on the fence of success or failure. Marguerite and I are soul mates. We have the same dreams and certainly have respected each other's decisions out of love and devotion because it meant something to us.

Humans are the kings of existence here on Earth. Yet we are as a human species always fighting, always causing large amounts of harm. Please continue with me on this journey, so you can understand my final conclusion and recommendations based on my experiences. Let's focus on how to create at will, the taste of hope.

CHAPTER

3

# WHEN PAIN COMES IN WORDS AND ACTIONS

Let's face it, some people simply don't think before they open their mouths.

Honestly, I am guilty of the same thing during different times in my life. I have embarrassed myself as well as others over the years for saying something foolish about someone when lo and behold that person is standing directly behind me.

What about some of the things that are said to you about your decisions when you are faced with a life-threatening ordeal? I have a few to share. I will also share my reflections in the end of what was probably the right way to address those individual issues. However, shock takes over and leaves a void between your brain and your mouth. I am usually paralyzed when hurtful stupid things are said to me. Mostly out of shock. Why would they say that to me? What were they thinking? Do they have a predetermined opinion that I am not a good person? That this was brought on by me or my wife? This feels and tastes like a verbal attack as though I don't have a clue, but their words are the words of wisdom that I must hear and digest.

The first 5 of my 28 years at the shipyard, I worked third shift. A graveyard shift, and we were never the popular crew. However, once married, I transferred to day shift. It wasn't an easy task as the foreman of my department blatantly told me when I approached him with my shop steward to request a transfer to day shift after 5 years on third shift. "I don't give a S#&t if you spend your life on the third shift. I need you there and that is final!! Now get out of my office". This was my first meeting with him. Nice huh? Talk about bringing out the best in people.

I went through labor relations and jumped through some hoops to be transferred to day shift. It was 2 years that I worked on a crew that I really enjoyed and bonded with. It was that time Kevin was diagnosed. I took a couple days of vacation to make a plan, and then I went to the foreman's office a second time. Oh, this ought to be good, I thought. No shop stewards this time, maybe that was my downfall. I approached the long countertop / chest high barrier that had a swing door on the left end for access into the supervisor's realm of desks. It looked like a teachers lounge in a way but with more chaos.

One of the assistant foremen came to the desk and asked "What do you want?"

"I need to talk to someone about a personal issue I have"

"What kind of *'Personal Issue'* do you have?" he asked in a mocking tone.

"My son was recently diagnosed with Leukemia last Friday. I just wanted to come in and see what I ..."

He stopped me by holding up one finger in the air. "We have a lost time policy here, you have to follow it, if you don't, you lose your job, it's that simple."

I was frozen. Thoughts were going through my head like an electrical storm. Insurance, wife, income, son, hospital costs, what did I do, I haven't missed any time yet. I stood there silent for what seemed like a long time, and then thankfully another assistant foreman overheard the conversation. His name – Bud Huer. He literally pushed the other assistant foreman away from the countertop and said. "Listen – go back and take care of your son. Keep in touch with your supervisor and we will work with you. Okay?"

I could barely get the word okay past my lips. The lump in my throat was huge, my heart was pounding in my chest which felt like it was going to explode. Someone with a heart and brain saw this issue for what it was. I then wanted to call out to the other assistant foreman and make some type of hand gesture or method of satisfaction to let him know I thought he was a complete ass. But I didn't. My job wasn't worth it. I later realized that Bud Huer was my supervisors' boss and he already knew my work ethic. I didn't take that lightly.

Next was a big one for us. Let's just say a family member called my wife while I was at work. The words of this person may have been spoken with good intent, but it hurt us like a stab in the heart with a spoon. The recommendation was that we leave Kevin at the hospital for the month. They have plenty of nurses that can care for him and we have another son at home who needs us. I learned of this upon coming home from work. I was on a vanpool from all the local townies that also worked at the shipyard that picked me up and dropped me off at the door amongst the other passengers. She had come home as we had only one vehicle. I was swapping with her on this Friday evening and I was going to spend the evening with Kevin at the hospital while she could be home. It is very taxing as a parent to sleep in the hospital room.

I found Marguerite sitting on the floor sobbing. It took me several minutes to calm her down so that she could be understood. She told me about the call, between breakdowns.

"What am I doing wrong?" she asked

"You are not doing anything wrong. You are his mother and Brian's mother. Together we will figure this out because you are not alone or doing a damn thing wrong".

It only took a moment of thought for me to encourage Marguerite to call this family member back. Her thoughts on the suggestion came flowing out, the lack of empathy for the situation but the sheer thought that leaving a child to face Leukemia alone with strangers seemed too cold to comprehend. She continued to share her feelings and her points were well spoken. Well, the returned call did not go over well. It actually caused quite a riff that I thought would never end. The family member dropped by at the hospital with spouse and kids in tow to wish Brian a happy birthday and to announce they were still going to Disney and not for us to expect them to cancel their plans because of us.

"No, by all means, go and enjoy yourself. We'll be just fine here" I said. The meeting was brief, and they departed. I never said anything besides those words, and it took several years for any relationship to form into something that felt comfortable. Nothing was ever resolved from it. It was simply ignored.

After a month of Kevin receiving chemotherapy and a second bone marrow sample, he was considered in remission. We brought him home and I, with a co-worker volunteer Mike Atwater, built a small deck and a staircase on our newly built house. These were not included with the contract as we wanted to keep costs down as much as possible. All signed in late Sept. so we could be as frugal as possible. A lot can happen in a few months that is for sure. We built these two accesses into the house before the due date bank inspection so that we could close on the house and move in. A very exciting time. We could not wait to get out of the apartment. There were 2 other people on the street that were diagnosed with Leukemia and a friend of Marguerite's who lived less than ½ mile from where we lived. Without proof, all we could go on is that we were spooked out and wanted to move.

Kevin came down with a blood infection in his central line which was the primary reason why he was frequently hospitalized. Low immune system due to Chemo–it was bound to happen, and it did. It was a week before Christmas, and we were afraid that we could possibly be spending Christmas in the hospital. The staff said it isn't a bad thing because Santa comes to every room and the kids are really spoiled. As sweet as that sounded, we wanted to be home as a family. Mind you that I didn't take more time off from work. This was before FMLA was passed. I was the only income and with the house going up, well, I worked the day shift, traveled to hospital to spend the evening with Kevin and to give Marguerite a break and to be with Brian. You guessed it if you were wondering. None of the family members who criticized us helped with watching Brian or went to sit at the hospital with Kevin.

In fact, one of the family members marched into the apartment the day after Christmas, our moving day. "I am here to inspect for damages." There were no damages we rebutted, but the self appointed or requested inspector had a job to do. Marguerite asked this family member if a lending hand of putting boxes in the moving truck were possible.

"It's your stuff not mine, move it yourself". I was not impressed by the practicing Catholic who says this one day after Christmas but hey, I am beginning to see what this person is really made of. The family members never apologized and certainly Marguerite wasn't going to apologize for defending herself.

A neighbor at our new home, who also had three kids all around Kevin and Brian's age, began to play with the boys. At the time Brian was a little older and they enjoyed the new found friendship. Marguerite was outside with the boys in the yard and the neighbor called her 3 children into their yard.

"Come over here and play in our yard. I don't want you getting cancer," she shouted out.

WHAT? Where the hell did that come from? Surely by now at the end of the 20$^{th}$ century we in the free world should know that cancer is not a communicable disease like the flu or Chickenpox. This was yet another challenge that we were slapped with.

So, Marguerite called this person on the phone and confronted the spoken words head on. "I heard you outside earlier when you said that you don't want your kids playing with mine because you don't want your kids catching cancer. I am calling to tell you that it doesn't work like that. It isn't contagious. I am really disappointed that you would treat my sons that way. I hope you can educate yourself to know that your fears are not valid," she told the neighbor, who was a school teacher.

I didn't see it at the time when I decided to propose marriage, but this was one of those proud moments that I knew she was the fantastic mother I thought she would be. We moved on and our kids played together, we had BBQ's and a beach day which was one of the most memorable times I held near and dear to my heart. But as all things occur, sometimes people simply drift away and that was the case here.

I think church was where I heard this next comment, from a parishioner. I was confused and angry and seeking something for a glimpse of understanding, why? As if I could find the answer to that in a 45 to 50 minute Catholic service. Many a morning I would sit in the pew and silently cry with tears rolling down my face with the complexity of thoughts I had running through my head, while I sought guidance from above.

I would take almost anything except this comment; "God doesn't give you anymore than you can handle". I am going to challenge you on that one – oh good and intending wise one who volunteers their elder experiences in hopes that I will be elated that I have been chosen by God as was my son to be stricken with this terminal disease so that I may know it will be okay. He knows I can handle it. Kevin – I am so sorry that I have strong convictions and that you were chosen by

God, it's all my fault that you have to experience the bone marrow samples and chemotherapy. I am the chosen one.

Nope! Short and simple. There are two different sides to everything, including faith. God has plans for you, which is a strong consideration for predestination. Yet there is also the belief amongst Christians that we were born to this earth with free will. We choose what we want when we want. This debate could go on for another few chapters. Some might say that I had to experience all that I have and am going through so that I can write this book and help many. If that is the case, I am honored that I was chosen but my follow up question is Why Me? There are no miracles like a burning bush that makes us see the relevance of something spectacular. However I do have a theory that I will share in my final chapter. It may just have a thread of attachment to the title.

How about the person who approaches you at the mall and says, "Hey, what's wrong with your kid?"

"Nothing is wrong with him. In fact we are really proud of him," we responded.

"Well, he lost his hair and he looks sick. What is it?"

"Leukemia – A.L.L. is the type he has," we calmly explained. "Oh yeah ? My sisters' brother-in-law's kid had Leukemia a few years back, yeah…. Looked as sick as your son does. He passed away. Good luck to you all." My depth of appreciation for that commentary, equals that of a surface puddle after a brief rain.

There are other things that have occurred that I have probably forgotten and honestly, that is a good thing. What I will tell you is that it leaves a scar on your soul. Yes the children's poem of Sticks and Stones has merit at times, but fails to address what words can actually do to a person.. Positive influences make everything better and negative comments hurt deeply.

Stop and reflect on a time in your life that you absolutely despise of something that was said to you. What were the scarring words that cut so deeply? Do you feel the scar in your soul still? What would make it better? Do you believe that God put you through that because he knew you could handle it? Hopefully you are not nodding your head yes to that last question as you are wiping away tears, as the scar has been acknowledged once again by your thought pattern and the pain is still there, it was just lying dormant.

Now let's take a couple of minutes to ponder what we are about to say and what repercussions words might have if they are spoken harshly or hurtfully. I learned a valuable skill from Dr. Gary Alligretta who was the third child oncologist at Maine Children's Cancer Program. To me he was brilliant, and his words and thoughts were formed with distinct calculation. I recall asking him a question in the presence of Marguerite in Kevin's hospital room. I can't recall what the exact question was, but I will say that is when my love and appreciation grew for this man and his approach to say things once and with thought behind it. Once the question was asked, he looked at me, and then Marguerite, then cast his gaze at the floor. He stared at the floor like he was in a trance or hypnotized. One minute passed, two minutes passed. We stood there watching him stare at the floor. I told him, look its okay if you don't know the answer, just …. "Wait – I'm thinking," he interrupted. He never moved his gaze from the floor and after another minute passed, he began to explain. He didn't shoot from the hip with a quick witted "I know everything" ego attitude. He plotted the whole question out and dissected it and built an answer on something that was worth a couple minutes of time. I had never seen that approach done again by anyone, yet I believe it should be done more often by many.

"Boy oh boy, I don't envy you" is another thought provoker. Why not say – "Wow your life really sucks and I am glad it is you and not me" Perhaps that could have been the 30 second- or 1-minute pause to think of a statement that makes understanding a little easier.

Rest assured that each situation that we have been through has changed me. It has opened my eyes to the individual, the so-called friend, the family member that was so counted on but looked the other way. The community and general population, the insurance companies as well as hospital staff. Health care / social workers and people who are simply afraid that your situation exists at all.

We have experienced joyful and happy days in our lives. Hopefully like me you have been able to have consecutive days of cheerful bliss. When you do, you find that cares and anxiety are at an all time low. Birds sound louder outside. They are actually singing beautifully. Have you noticed how the sun feels upon your face and skin? A warm blanket of light is upon you. It feels rejuvenating to your soul. Laughter comes easier. TV commercials are funny to watch. Engaging in conversation with people comes more naturally.

When deep pain sits atop of your soul there is nothing that appears funny. A snide comment or something that is a little bit of a poke to joke with you feels more like an insult and an attack than a friendly quip. If those words were spoken on a day that was joyful instead of foreboding, then the playful banter may arise. Jokingly it may turn into a "Well your mother is so fat" joke because you can identify with that degree of humor since you are in a great mood. Have the weight of the world on your mind and shoulders and it could mean that you may do or say something that you regret.

    I recall working at the shipyard in a small building where we performed sandblasting and painting of items. When we usually finished one special application of coating it had to be stenciled with 3 letters. This remained until the final coat was applied. Well I was bringing a daily newspaper to work with me from home. We were banking on our one income and a daily newspaper was something that was about all I could afford for myself. I valued that paper as something that I could enjoy reading a little at coffee break as well as lunch. Well one morning I returned to the break area to find that my newspaper had been stenciled over with the three letters. The front, the back page, a couple of internal pages. SNAP went my brain.

    I was so deep in the forest of depression that I snapped. I grabbed the paper and began yelling at the top of my lungs, "Who stenciled my personal newspaper? My voice was coming deep from within my diaphragm. I could feel my face turning red. It felt flush and at one point I started seeing stars. I shouted repeatedly with some very strong adjectives and obscenities. Stares were upon me. Fear crossed some of their faces, however I did not feel like anyone was brave enough to raise their hand to say "It was me."

    I gave up and threw my newspaper away. I felt like my own personal possession of a newspaper couldn't go without someone tampering with it. Joke or no joke, I was offended that I could be a target when I already felt like a target with my son's illness. "Anyone want my lunch too? Want to take that?" I asked with deep sarcasm. I said it as I thought, go ahead and try taking my lunch you #%@ !%&#.

It was probably 14 years later that I was at a birthday celebration and a lobster feed. One of the sandblasters was there and out of the blue he looked at me and said; "I remember that day when you lost it because someone stenciled your newspaper." I was shocked and embarrassed that this event made a lasting impression on him of a time that I was at one of my lowest moments. "You really shocked me when you did that and I never understood why you flew off like that, I mean you really lost it over nothing."

CHAPTER

4

# LOVE, LAUGHTER AND FINDING YOUR POWER MOTIVATION

There we were as a young couple just starting out. Twenty-seven years old with two boys at two years and nine months respectively. We were emotionally paralyzed from this diagnosis and had barely enough motivation to make decisions with clarity. Maybe this was something that was only happening to us. There was another couple whose son was diagnosed almost a month after Kevin. They were the nicest people. Upbeat, happy, unphased by this detour in life. They stayed positive and appeared to face this as though it was a broken leg, with some hospital time. Perhaps they took it for its face value when the doctor said their son had a solid chance in beating this. Marguerite and I were complete skeptics.

There were caring people that would ask – What can I do to help? Honestly, we didn't know what to tell them. I had never been through anything like this before. Up to that point the most difficult thing I had been faced with was helping decide who we can put at a table for the wedding reception so everyone would get along and enjoy themselves. Then Kevin asked to go home. It wasn't so much about us as it was for him. This little guy had his body invaded by pain. So we told him he was sick with some germs and had to stay in the hospital for a little while. To a two-year-old a month seems like half a lifetime. So I would tell those who wanted to help that I would let them know when I did.

We considered St. Jude's Hospital. Memphis, Tennessee is a long way from Maine, and we were told that there would be complications at times where Kevin would have to be hospitalized. It would be extremely difficult for us and risky for him since he would be immunocompromised. Our hospital worked directly with Boston children's hospital as well as another one in Paris, France. They acted as a collaborative team with Maine Children's and were doing great things. We didn't have to think much about staying close to home after hearing that rational explanation.

The first two weeks I wouldn't have been surprised if we were nicknamed the zombie parents. We looked pathetic. We wore our emotions on our sleeves. Sadness and depression grabbed us. I knew we had to do something, but I could not spend my time lifting Marguerite up, worrying about Kevin, and going to work to ensure I kept my job. Marguerite walked away from her job upon the diagnosis. She openly admitted she would not be able to function at work and felt her duty lay with being beside our son. We mutually agreed that she would stop working and that I was going to "be the provider".

I took the first few days off from work with the remainder of vacation that I had. But it wasn't a full week. The company I worked for was a shipbuilding company. Contracts for the U.S. Navy to build naval ships. I went to work on the first Thursday and Friday of his first week of induction. It was agonizing. My stomach, my mind, my willpower and ability to function were all suffering. However, I was the sole income provider for the family. There were three people depending on me. I had to get it together somehow. Push the mental distractions aside by blocking them out.

There may be those in countries that are reading this book and thinking – "Why didn't he stay home too?" We did not have the type of insurance that would substitute my income. Since we are not part of a socialist society, we did not have any support. Remember the year was 1990 and the Family Medical Leave Act still was not enacted. It would not be enacted for another 3 years. So, I had to work.

But what about fundraisers? Someone put together a collection on our behalf at work. I was unaware of this collection as it was going on. I worked on a small, specialized crew in a workplace of perhaps 7 thousand people. It was and still is a unionized shipyard. One day I was approached by a shop steward. He explained to me that a collection was assembled on our behalf and that he was sorry for what we were going through. I was stunned and speechless. I humbly thanked the shop steward, and he turned and left me standing alone with a card in my hand. I wasn't sure if I should open it now or wait until I got home or to the hospital to share this with my family. I decided to open it. I carefully opened the card wondering what the contents were, what the message was. After all this wasn't something that I requested. No, this came from the heart of my coworkers, a workforce of several thousand people. I was choked up and could barely hold back the tears of emotions while I stood there opening the card. I drew it out and from there, I opened the card. The message was simple, and thoughtful. Sorry you are going through this. Our prayers are with you. Included in with the card was $42.00.

I'll be honest, I was stunned. It felt like a kick in the stomach, or perhaps a little lower. Yet those who contributed had a huge heart and gave because it meant something to them. It was then that I realized I was on this journey alone with my wife. Why should it be anyone else's problem, right? I was unknown to most of these people, and even the several hundred in the paint department for which I worked. I had a small crew that I worked with. I was not a popular person there, more like a wallflower. There were some that were outspoken as union members, or hosted amazing parties, or dozens of other things. Me, I simply kept to myself so my story didn't matter because nobody could identify with me. Later in the years the union started gate collections for those in need. I donated when I could, but often did not. Mainly because I was strapped for money and never carried cash. I did often reflect that the $42.00 was good intention and not made to insult me and my family. The value came not in the worth of the money, but in the internal reflection of someone who had to become an independent island. A rock if you will. Was I a rock before this? No, I would say not. My parents raised me to always be polite. My father taught me not to start a fight but to finish it. Old school values. I was not one to speak ill of anyone. When I started working third shift, I had a few crew members that would ridicule me and tell me that I would make someone a good wife someday. I ignored them. There must have been something about my personality that said, "Hey there is someone who is different, he is not like the rest of us. Let's harass him and see what he is made of". I'd had my share of harassment throughout school, and now it was going to be part of my work life.

Following my father's teachings about fighting, I was once riding on a bus home from school in the fourth grade. We lived in Virginia Beach at the time as my father was in the navy. This boy in my neighborhood was sitting in front of me, turned around and told me to shut up. Everyone was talking, and I thought he was telling this to the person who was sitting next to me. I told him – turn around – everyone is talking on the bus. A few minutes went by and he spun around for a second time. Now he was angry, commanding, "I said shut up!" and he punched me twice in the face. I recall standing up and punching him back. That is all I recall. Apparently, I punched his face until they pulled me off of him. He was taken to the hospital as there was fear of eye damage from the beating. Nope – I only remember 2 punches.

I stopped fighting at that point. Although there have been some other altercation, but I was afraid of who was inside of me that took over and controlled me, of what was going on during the blackout. I never told people of this, because there was a fear that they would want proof. There would be this experiment to see exactly what I would do. I am nothing of a fighter though I have been in other conflicts, but I try to keep my composure. Always trying to stay away from redlining.

Why am I mentioning this? I needed this job, and the benefits of health insurance. The first month of Kevin's hospital stay was $72,000.00 dollars and we had 1 year, and 11 months left of his protocol treatment. Whatever anger that built inside of me for what my son was experiencing, along with my wife, I needed to direct and focus on my own. The medical insurance I had through work covered most if not all of his medical bills. I could do nothing to jeopardize that, ever.

Have you had an outburst, or gone from passive to aggressive without justification? Then the embarrassment and humiliation set in? You may never know what people around you are thinking, but trust me, they are thinking something about your outburst. It is a terrible situation to be in. Emotions are running high. You, like me, may feel increased anxiety and fear. Then the voice in your head kicks in. You know what voice I mean. Your conscience, that voice that you think is your thinking mind. Yeah…that one. It took me a lifetime not to listen to everything that voice said. It wasn't until I reached my 50's that I stumbled on an author – Eckhart Tolle. He describes that voice in your head as an ego that is craving attention.

However, I digress. Let's go back to the second week of Kevin's month-long induction of chemotherapy. This month was a full court press of bombarding his body with chemotherapy with the end goal of placing him in remission. What is remission? In layman's terms it is when signs and symptoms of the cancer are not present, however it could still be hiding. It was then that my world was coming to a dark and abrupt reality. I drove the 37 miles from work to the hospital as an attentive, yet exhausted young man. I was using my fathers second vehicle so Marguerite could drive our car at will. I arrived at his room, kissed my wife who was attending to Kevin and Brian while I was away. I picked Kevin up from the hospital crib as he wore his hospital Johnny PJ's. As I lifted him from the crib, I felt the magnitude of his weight loss. He was light as a feather. His breath was that of medicine and stale morning breath. His eyes were sunken and dark. I had seen that before. Typically, on a movie or TV show when someone was on their deathbed. I held him as tight as I could. Oh my God, I am losing him, I thought. He is wasting away and would be dead soon.

I looked at Marguerite and asked how much weight he'd lost, or what his weight was now. It was a few pounds from what the nurse reported. I closed my eyes and held him. It was then that I knew I would not lose our son without a fight. I refused to allow this child to feel afraid. Life should be filled with love, and happiness. That thought felt like any positive analogy that you can imagine. I turned to Marguerite and said; "this stops here, this stops right now". She looked at me with puzzled fear.

"Wallowing in all this medical depression. We should be concentrating on demonstrating love and happiness," I said.

"Do you feel better when there is happiness around when you're sick? Depression is obviously a downer, so why do we allow this into our lives? They say he has a chance of beating this, so let's make him happy. Let's make everyone happy and realize that love will be the binding glue that keeps him healthy as well as a better chance of a cure.

Yes, right out of a movie right? Seriously, I thought, is she really going to buy this? Yes, it was a great motivational speech, but we had been zombies for the past two weeks. How were we simply going to go in the other direction and take charge? I wasn't sure, but the two-year-old in my arms was enough of a motivator. I knew we owed it to him as parents.

It was then that Marguerite and I began looking for means of inspiration. I will tell you this, inspiration is like a favorite color. It may not be the same for every person. I used to have a favorite color, but at some earlier point in my life I realized that my favorite color depends upon what it is displaying. I love green grass or fields, but green isn't my favorite color. A clear blue sky is not only amazing when not a single cloud is displayed, yet blue is not my favorite color. Red perhaps? Well, it looks amazing on a dress which is wrapped around a beautiful woman. But they all are not my favorites. I appreciate all colors. Therefore, I should embark on looking for multiple means of inspiration for love and humor. There were no physics or chemistry courses needed. Just seeking multiple things that will inspire love, inspire humor. Enjoying life whenever possible

Perhaps the biggest problem is that I am a quiet introvert compared to a lot of people. I must work, not in the labor of having a job but in a way that earns the depth of my family's love and happiness. It is a cold bare fact that we assume to be a given. Yet there are some fathers, mothers, husbands or wives who are barely participating in the lives that they share with their spouse or children. I work at my words that are spoken, my actions and support. They all matter to the recipient. Not a big deal you might think.

Early TV shows depicted strong family values. How to properly resolve a difficult situation. There have even been attempts for empathy like the movie Philadelphia with Tom

Hanks who plays a man that contracted aids. There are so many things going on in the world, but there is no guidebook or movie to show the example of what to do as a parent of a child with cancer. Nor is there a movie that helps the friends, neighbors, or family help those who are going through the nightmare. So, at any given time someone reflects on your situation and thinks it is sad, I'm uncomfortable with seeing them in this state. I am going to give them their private time, give them the space they deserve, you would be doing them an extreme disservice. Turns out it comes with a lot of other illnesses that people find to stay away from.

Perhaps if they were to notice that your personality has changed and they are uncomfortable about it, please do not try to appease their comfort. What is really required is that you and your immediate family be true to yourselves. Do not deny your emotions like fear, anger, despair, sadness. This is what you are experiencing, and this is your life in these very trying times. If others see this is affecting you and your personality, then be proud of that. You are adapting to this new challenge of life. We all must grow and change as life continues. We should never cower before what we are dealt with. The one emotion I caution you not to hold onto is anger and resentment. I view it as the demon that falls upon us when we are weak. It creates a cloud of anguish that we believe can be expunged if we allow the anger to vent out and solve the situation for us. Undirected anger is the "go to fix" for most people. Please focus on yourself and seek help instead. A friend, a professional counselor, whatever, but never allow this to go unmanaged. There is much more to come in the following chapters regarding tactics and means to address what you are experiencing.

CHAPTER

# 5

# WHAT INSPIRES YOU TO KEEP GOING

There are so many influences in our lives that can make us happy or sad. We have days that are multi-tasking to the nth degree and yet there are days when we can't even move out of our own way to get something done. Combine that with the challenge of fighting cancer and you get what I consider mental gridlock. Traffic within a city's busy rush hour can really develop a sense of "I'm not getting anywhere" thinking. "Should I be on a different street that would move faster? What if I found a place to park and walked or took the subway?"

Then comes the short breathing, the anxiety rising in your mind and tightness in your stomach or chest. Hostility combined with frustration as you find yourself speaking out loud, which then transfers into an abrupt shout out within the confines of your vehicle as though whomever you are directing that vocal assault at can hear you and will move at your command. Vulgar words are shouted. Hand gestures flailing while you nervously watch the time and realize you are going to be late. Then, and only then does the imaginative onslaught of visions appear in your mind. The boss, the colleague, the spouse waiting for you. "Where have you been? I've been waiting for you. My God, I thought you forgot the appointment, blew me off, was in an accident, you weren't in an accident, were you? NO? Good…… WHERE WERE YOU, You're late!!!"

Well as paralyzing as depression is, it also has a significant impact on your day-to-day life. It can impair your cognitive thinking, concentration as well as memory. Well that is just great isn't it? Not only are you faced with a major challenge in your life, but the depression it causes holds you back as well. Getting out of that rut can be as challenging as deciding to go to college in midlife, do a turn around and lose weight that you have been holding onto, proposing a total career change. You get the picture right? I am speaking from experience, however what goes on between my ears and between my lungs emotionally is a lot different than what's on the surface.

Look, I'll be honest, I didn't make it look like it was all a walk in the park. I wear my emotions on my sleeve. It was much worse when I was in my late 20's. Combine being raised in an emotionally sideways family setting with parents that viewed things from a non-supportive outlook. I mean that with all the deepest love and respect for both of my parents. Challenges like childhood leukemia with our son, a brain tumor with my wife, encephalitis with our second son, we were living a life where suggestions or recommendations didn't come without pain.

"You hang in there. God doesn't give you anymore than you can handle." This phrase as I mentioned in a previous chapter is one of my least favorite slogans of inspiration. Really? So this is all God's plan?

What I have concluded from years of contemplating this theory is this. God created man and earth along with the Universe. We were given the freedom of free will. I was struggling with knowing why. I prefer free will over having a dictator for a God. His love and compassion combined with forgiveness is tremendous and is the only thing that changes lives for the better. I never challenged the advice from the person offering the words, God doesn't give you more than you can handle. After all, they were trying. Perhaps they heard it from someone else and thought it sounded inspirational.

My mother taught me to always be nice to people. Say please and thank you. Don't talk back and certainly don't be rude by saying things that would hurt someone's feelings. Words hurt and can carry through your mind for the rest of your life. Depending on your sensitivity or how you hold onto the words that are presented to you, there may be a rabbit hole that you go down occasionally. You know what I am talking about. The quiet, still times in your day or workweek. Those moments when you have reflection time or when your mind slows down enough from your day that it starts popping up with random thoughts. No, you don't feel the pain of stubbing your toe barefoot on that coffee table from seven years ago, but those words that someone cut into your mind and soul are definitely coming back to haunt you. Usually when you least expect it. It is my idle time that brings the painful memories forward. I try to fill my time with thoughts that are occupying and not idle.

The reality of it is our culture in the United States rarely has social philosophers. Those who can offer words of wisdom that bring sense to our troubled times. The more things happened to us, the more I wondered – what did I do to deserve this? What do you think happened to my depression? Well it didn't get any better that is for sure. What I did to solve this was to stay busy. I would get up at 4 in the morning, go to work at the shipyard and bury myself in it. I used it as a distraction from my thoughts. If my brain was busy working, it couldn't or simply wouldn't have the time to contemplate the situation my family was in.

I became a "workaholic" and a "clock racer". I was good at it. I would stack up my work load and challenge myself to see how much I could accomplish, and how much I could do tomorrow. It proved to be a distraction and an addictive life pattern. I never ran, or appeared to be frantic. But everything I did was a race to see what I could do to shave time off my accomplishment. Not just in work, but the 'challenge to do something epic that no one else has done' sort of thing. So, being a father, husband, homeowner and needing to fill my time some more, I chose to challenge myself to a monumental task of climbing a mountain in Maine. I rode in a vanpool with a guy by the name of Levitt. We discussed Mt. Katahdin a few times and decided to make plans to do it. But it wasn't next door. We both agreed that we didn't have time to take an entire weekend and the desire to do this feat was becoming stronger and stronger. So, one July Saturday morning at 0230 a.m. I picked him up at his apartment and we drove the 3 hours to Millinocket Maine.

It was there that we began the 4000 ft. ascent to the peak on the longest and most difficult trail. Knife'sEdge takes 8 to 12 hours to complete. Once you have made it to the peak, you have limited time to make it down any trail before dark. Once done, we made it back to the car in the parking lot around 5:30 – 6 pm and drove home.

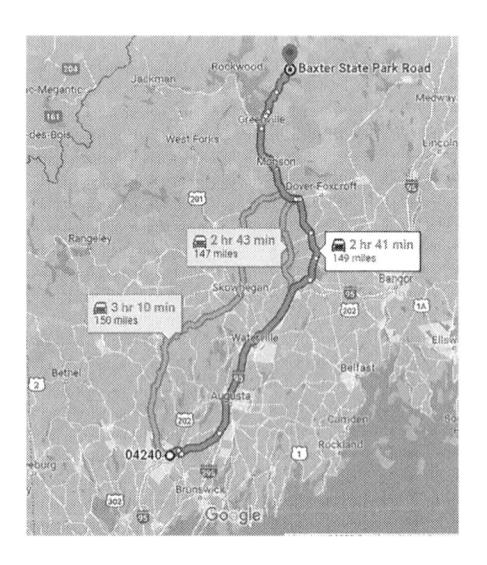

So did my obsessive behavior of trying to fit everything into one day fix my situation? No, it did not. It only bolstered the twisted belief that I was forging a path in my life where I was able to do the outer limits of what I was capable of accomplishing. I never faced my emotions. People depended on me. My wife, and our three sons. I was like a lot of people, always trying to show my parents that I was a self-sufficient adult and could handle anything that came my way in life. That lie I told myself and attempted to pass off to others may or may not have been believed.

The fact is we all play a role in our families, our social circles, and community. We act the part that we think is important to feel we are received. In control, confident, we have values that are unwavering to a fault. I don't have all the answers but I have the love of God, Country and my family in my heart. Pretty patriotic as a human on the planet huh? Well, I am here to tell you that we are all going to break. We may have a strong face and an image of "wow, that person (man or woman) really has their shit together. I couldn't do what they were doing. I would crumble.

I am writing this to tell you that you will crumble, as I have many times. I sometimes hear the accolades: "I so admire what he has done to stand by his family and to go through all that he has without falling off the deep end." Not true. I have not only fallen off the deep end but have been so far down that rabbit hole that I forgot there was a sun and stars above me. I simply pretended for years to play the part. To act like I had a master plan, I executed it, and look at me now.

You know when something is wrong when you watch a movie, or popular TV show that everyone in your circle of people that you talk to says that TV show is an absolute riot, and when you watch it there is no humor found in it at all. This went on for several years. If there was laughter around me from a joke or situational humor, I would pretend to laugh so I fit in. I wasn't an idiot. I knew that if I didn't laugh, I would be considered a "lump on a log", a "killjoy". I wanted to be funny in the worst way because in our society we love to be around people who make us laugh. They get invited to parties and are often asked to hang out with groups of people at a dinner or social event. It didn't matter. I couldn't hold that line for long. I retreated into the social introvert that I have always been. I let the extrovert out every once in a while, for some exercise.

My introverted personality's internal strength required some recharging. What was it going to be? I had a lot going on and had no hobbies. I wanted a hobby but nothing interested me. I tried reading, but I always felt guilty when I was reading that I should be doing something else. Work is being missed because I am reading for pleasure instead of attending to tasks. I know, I know, that is a special kind of stupid thought system, but honestly I didn't know how to relax.

You may or may not be aware that the DC character Superman's energy and strength is recharged, not by the fortress of solitude, but the sun itself. When he was weak he needed to be in the sunlight to recharge him. I did not have a clue until I was driving to work one day and heard a song on the radio. I had heard it before, but I heard it differently this time. Phil Collins released "In the air tonight" in 1981, the year my wife and I graduated from high school. Here I am in 1990 and am listening to this with an entirely different ear of intent. This song's lyrics were sung in my head as though it were me confessing that I have seen death and what it does to children with cancer. It is now that I am face to face with death and its lies regarding Leukemia. Leukemia has a tendency to fool the medical field as well as parents with pretending to look like something else. A cold, flu, bronchitis, and a host of other things. So if I saw "death" drowning – I would not lend a hand. "I've seen your face before my friend but I don't know if you know who I am," sings Phil Collins. "I was there, I saw what you did, I saw it with my own two eyes. So you can wipe off that grin, I know where you've been. It's all been a pack of lies."

This is where I pictured I was standing before death like in the Lord of the Rings book where Gandalf stands against the Balrog on the stone bridge in Moria. But instead of saying "You shall not pass," I was defying death by saying "YOU CANNOT HAVE HIM"

"You have to go through me first and you are going to be sorry I got out of bed this morning." Foolish and silly as it sounds, when that song played on the radio that is all I thought of, and a lot of times when I was driving I either changed the channel or turned it down if someone else was in the car with me, or I turned it up while driving along yelling the lyrics until I had to pull over because I could no longer see the road through my tears. "Yes, the hurt doesn't show, but the pain still grows, it's no stranger to you and me," then the epic drum fill drives my adrenaline and determination into the sunlight upon Superman's face. THERE ! I will beat this as I protect my family. That is all I needed.

I felt at times God or my guardian angel knew when it was time for me to hear that song. I couldn't simply play it once a day on a cassette deck (yeah that's right a cassette deck). No this came at the times when I didn't see it coming, but was feeling low and boom, I was back in the game. Just so you know, reader of this book, it took me over an hour to write this one paragraph because after 30 years, I still break down and cry when I review the lyrics and thoughts of my past. Emotional pain runs far deeper than physical. It is what we do with it that makes us or breaks us. You have the ability to rise above it.

Find that song be it country, rock, classical, rap, and when you feel that burning within your soul that props you up and says to your inner spirit "You've got this" then make note. You are on your path to being on top. You have the ability to be your inspiration when only you know what is needed within your soul to build a repair center in your heart. To forge an army of one and show the world you have it under control. Music releases dopamine which is a chemical that aids in you feeling good, happy.

To have control over your situation, your spirit and thoughts you must realize that you can only control the present moment. It has been said so many times in our culture, with little attention to its value, I think it falls on deaf ears to many. "You cannot change the past, the future isn't here yet, you can only have the Now which is a gift, and that is why they call it the present."

Sweet words when you can see the value of the phrase. So why do we have such a difficult time practicing it. We continue to lunge toward our future. We use the 'now' with such disregard. It is obvious that the word "we" can be exchanged with "I" in this descriptive paragraph. I must concentrate on the now. For the past 3 years I have been making many attempts to do so.

An author who has incredible insight on what goes on in our minds and hearts as people is Eckhart Tolle. I have listened to his two books – "The New Earth" and "The Power of Now" over and over. He provides me with a grounding stillness that centers my internal rage and anger when the world disappoints me. Depression as well as what he calls the voice in your head is a force that can jar your confidence, make you doubt those around yourself and fail before you start. We all should take time to look within ourselves and visit the stillness that our minds long for. This is why vacations are important. Hobbies are a distraction for us to decompress and let the world that we live in step aside.

Therefore, when you can, seek the silent moments of non-thinking, without sleep. Staring at a fire in a fireplace, campfire or a wood stove seems to draw you in and you feel mesmerized by the three-dimensional flames dancing. You are experiencing a moment of non-thinking. Yes, thoughts will rush into your mind, pay attention. These are thoughts that do not constantly occupy your mind. I believe this is why we enjoy sitting by a fire so much. We feel mentally rejuvenated afterwards. It wasn't just the company you kept, it wasn't the alcohol that you consumed while sitting around the fire. You can receive the same effect and perhaps more if you viewed the fire alone. It was your brain realizing it released endorphins because it received a break from thinking. It was visually stimulated by the dancing flames that triggered a sense of relaxation and self-centering.

Candles may offer the same, however it is more of a background distraction to relax your brain. It does create a light that is soothing and relaxing, often associated with a romantic mood or perhaps used in a religious manner. Yet the candle flame has those mesmerizing properties as well.

Electronics have become a distraction of epidemic proportions. I am not just a critic, I am a victim as well. Back when our son was fighting his illness of Leukemia, computers were just making their way into the home of society. Now we can do so much with our phones it really doesn't seem practical at times to have a computer. Banking, bill paying, social media, stock market monitoring, games, health apps and the list just simply goes on and on. The internet is at our fingertips. We panic when we lose or misplace our phones. Now there seems to be a hierarchy of importance to which people want to communicate with people. Calls, text messages, social media instant messages. Those who have broken hearts or a family member going through something that is life threatening deserve more than a text or an instant message saying, "thinking of you" or "prayers and hugs". We often feel as though we are surviving underwater somehow. Able to steal a breath of air to survive while we are fighting cancer, the life-threatening illness that is draining us of our energy through worry and fear. To experience the visual changes and those moments of doubt that drive a knife into your heart. Text messages don't do it. Instant messages or memes on Facebook are not going to make that go away.

I can honestly say there are but a handful of people in my life that would actually trust that prayer occurred for any situation that we were in. Yet I felt nothing from those prayers. I didn't feel more energy as though I just awoke from a much-needed nap. If you want to do something that makes a difference, then "Go and See". A common term used in my current job. If we cannot determine what the problem is, then we must "Go and See" for ourselves. What difference can that make you ask? It takes the loneliness out of someone's day. It enables a conversation to occur that is perhaps something outside of the worry that someone has for their situation. Bring them a meal. Share with them that meal or simply drop it off saying "I hope this gives you some free time to do something for you instead of cooking and cleaning up."

It causes depression and anxiety to face a life-threatening event. Paralyzing actions take over the person who is holding up the walls around themselves. No one can fix this situation with the exception of the doctors and nurses. You want a miracle? Be thankful that there are people who are inspired by whatever force that whispers to them to follow a passion and specialty that they have done. Be it the Holy Spirit, guardian angels, God, Mohammed, Buddha or whatever religious figure that we follow.

There was a fire of passion to pursue the depth of education for these people to help. They are doing their job and helping with science, bringing hope. It is the friends and family members that have to be brave and stand up to say, I am going to do something to help.

People used to ask my wife and I, "what can we do to help"? Remember that phrase of paralyzed fear I spoke of?

When people asked us what we needed, we only wanted a cure. That was a gut-wrenching response for people to hear because they couldn't help with that. Then they too would become paralyzed with not knowing what to do. Then the distance grew stronger and stronger. Alone again and facing a long-term dire situation that you are forced to contend with while it seems the entire world around you is functioning just fine. People are laughing, going out to parties, having a great time.

So aside from the music that you chose as a fight song, an inspirational photo that speaks to you or a movie that depicts a hero in a terrible situation that you somehow identify with, reach down into your heart and identify something that would lift your spirit. "I'd like to go out to a park alone sometime so that I can perhaps gather some thoughts uninterrupted" "I'd really like to have you stop by and have lunch with me more often, I really value you being in my life and I enjoy our time together" "I don't know what I need or want but I know I don't want to be alone, can you stay with me and help me figure it out?"

I think that people look at a situation based on how their life is going right now. The free time they have, the lack of a depressive state. Their own health is a big one. Don't criticize someone's choices unless you are willing to spend a week with them. Follow them in their daily life. Watch but do not judge the decisions they make and problems they are faced with. We all have different experiences in this world. We also have different levels of cognition and intelligence. After the week, or at the very best, listening to the details of a couple full days. Then multiply that out per week and month, seasons and years. Now go back and offer something that is substantial to that person. Holding a hand, offering to have a girls night out.

Ignore them when it matters and don't be shocked when you are ignored. Friends are there through the good times and bad. If it doesn't measure up to that level. If your friendship means that in the middle of the night you are willing to go and help someone in need. Then you are simply an acquaintance. Perhaps a shallow friendship at best. I think the world is a bit messed up and we deserve to have a change. We deserve to right the ship. Currently we are so independent in this world that it becomes second nature to help. Instead, try nurturing the taste of hope. Make it sweet and creamy. Prevent bitterness from being the dominant taste of hope. There is enough of that in the world.

CHAPTER

6

# CONGRATULATIONS – TOGETHER, YOU HAVE BEAT CANCER

So, it was in November of 1990 when our son was diagnosed with Acute Lymphoblastic Leukemia or ALL. 2 years of chemotherapy followed by a third year with starting his protocol all over again. 1 month of induction followed by spinals and a full year of chemo as well as the infamous cranial radiation. Then when all was said and done, a few years of monitoring to see if it would come back on its own. Cancer cells can hide and be very very elusive. All it takes is for it to begin to grow and split once again, then 2 become 4, 4 becomes 16 and so on. "Time will tell so watch for the signs that you spotted back in 1990 such as unexplained bruising, getting a cold or any illness and not being able to fight it off easily. Watch for those energy dips. You remember those, wanting to take a nap or sleep in, never having energy to do much. Yes, watch for those for 4 to 5 years. In the meantime, we will do some routine checkups, blood work at the most and monitor his progress."

Then came that long awaited day. It really seemed so far out of reach as the new normal was being psychologically pushed into our lives that we must face this cancer battle for a lifetime. Others have, and still do. There are basically 5 types of leukemia and statistically we had the easiest to combat, regardless of being a "recall family".

We entered a new facility, which was moved for the third time during our treatment duration. A beautiful medical building where the practice truly deserved to be located. Seeing the staff of familiar faces and the love and respect that we developed for these brave people that go to work every day to see the faces of families battling the issues of their children day in and day out. It happened way before this day that we realized angels come in the form of people who are inspired to do this type of work for a living. A calling that makes more than a subtle difference in someone's day, but affects the future of an individual or family. I have the greatest respect for all who choose pediatric oncology as a career, for the nurses as well as for the nursing and clerical staff. Everyone has such a life saving role in their own domain and without one or the other, the success of a family is at risk.

We sat in the waiting room awaiting the callout for Kevin, then to be escorted to an exam room we were in high anxiety. Then, it happened; "Kevin". We stood up and immediately began walking in the direction of the nurse who called us. We were brought to a small conference room, not an exam room. We were asked to sit down and offered water, coffee or anything else to drink. The doctor came in, sat down and brought Kevin's immensely thick file with him. I dare say this file could challenge most phone books for the heavyweight title. But it really made sense. Document after document covering hospital stay after hospital stay. Medical procedures like bone marrow samples, cranial radiation, spinals, central line infections and replacements. All captured and documented.

What wasn't captured was the heartache of the parents' enduring of pre-diagnosis observations, 15 pediatric visits knowing something was wrong with our child's health only to be turned away with a diagnosis of; it's a flu bug that is going around. It is a touch of bronchitis, but he will bounce back. Kids get bruises but it really shouldn't be anything to worry about, and the list goes on. Diagnosis and the wonderment of "what did I do to cause this"? We both wondered if we were partially to blame. I worked in a shipyard and moreover was exposed to epoxy paints, solvents etc. I worked with a chemical called Trichloroethane 1,1,1. We used it specifically for degreasing metal. It was banned because it was an ozone depleting contributor not something that can act on someone's central nervous system.

Marguerite also cried at night wondering what we did to cause this, why couldn't we protect our son. The huge medical file would not depict the discrimination of neighbors not allowing their children to play with him. Nor did it prepare us for the nurse at the hospital who was attending to Marguerite and our third born son Shawn and her reaction when I brought Kevin and Brian over to the hospital to meet their new brother. She stepped into the room, took one look at our bald, sunken eyed son sitting on the bed with his mother and immediately turned away only to send someone else in. Clearly her issue and inability to deal with acting on this.

So the doctor came into the small conference room and greeted us with a happy yet neutral attitude. "Let's take a look and see what we have here," he said. I personally think this was a display of an evaluation for us. The real matter of this is decided by a panel of doctors, and a board that evaluates his case as much as we were evaluated to be a recall family. The file was thumbed through, skipped over sections and closed with little drama or conclusive finger pointing to a page.

"Well Mom, Dad .... Kevin, it looks like you beat Leukemia. Kevin – your chance of getting Leukemia is as good as mine are, or your parents or anyone on the street. It is gone. You've all beat it," he said with joyful conviction.

"No!" my wife said "You beat it, you and your team of angels beat this for us."

"Thank you for that" he humbly responded, "but we also know that good rest, a good diet, and the most important ingredient to fighting an illness is Love. You provided that all. These were the things that we could not do with day-to-day, hour by hour devotion like you both offered. It was you two. We just provided the medication." Pause in the room of awkward silence. "Congratulations" he concluded.

That's it, we were just told we had the winning numbers for the lottery. It hit us in that very same way. What do we do? Who do we call? EVERYONE!!! We have to celebrate, we have to make a huge deal out of this.

We arrived home, made phone calls, and went out to celebrate. We celebrated and rejoiced each time we woke up, each time we saw Kevin coming home from school or doing something he enjoyed. This was also met with deep, deep respect for those families that we got to know at Maine Children's Cancer Program. Those families that we would see at the hospital, or at the Sebago Lake camp for families to celebrate and bond. We were part of a dozen families that were diagnosed within a years' time. Kevin was one of three survivors of that group. My heart continues to mourn and cry for those families. I know the pain never goes away because the memory can return and wake you in your sleep, make you cry over a song.

What doesn't kill you makes you stronger, the old saying goes. Well, I think those words were formed by people who were part of an ordeal. They feel victorious in saying that. I believe it is reserved for those who have experienced the anguish of pain, regardless of whether it was cancer, being a prisoner of war, abduction etc. Not for that neighbor to mutter when they don't know what else to say. Not for the aunt or second cousin to say at Thanksgiving or some other get together. An elders wisdom should be in the form of love and support while listening to our stories of trials.

A day and weekend of living on a high that has no ceiling. My world was three dimensional. I saw the world differently. My life situation was a chapter ending while a new one is beginning. Beginning for all of us. Millions of dollars were not worth what we were feeling. How could it be?

Labor day came and school started. Marguerite worked in the school system in the next town over from ours. A river divided the two. She was an educational tech. Her skill was to help children who had reduced grade scores in reading. She was excellent at it too. The boys began their schooling, with the exception of Shawn, who was still in daycare. One week after Labor Day weekend, Marguerite decided that it might be time for Shawn to get his first eye exam. Obviously, it was something she set up prior to the exam date, as walk-in appointments for exams are a thing of the past, if they ever existed at all.

I was on my way home from working at the shipyard. When I arrived, my neighbor came to the house and said that Marguerite was at the eye doctor with Shawn. There was something wrong, she wouldn't say what it was, but called her to come and pick up Shawn, and let you know she is still there. The optometrist office was about a mile and a half away. When I arrived, I asked the front desk clerk where my wife was after giving her my name. She told me what exam room she was in and I immediately rushed there only to find my wife crying with a handful of tissues in her hand. I asked her what happened, what was going on?

"Shawn was nervous to sit in the chair in this dark room. The optical equipment was intimidating and he thought something was going to hurt him, so I sat in the chair to show him what was going to be expected in his eye test. I covered my left eye and read the letters, then I covered my right eye and the letters were gone. I told the nurse to turn the light back on and she said it is on. I cannot see the chart with my left eye. But I see fine without covering it.

Then the doctor came in and I introduced myself. It only took a brief second or two before he began speaking. "We believe that one of three things might have taken place. First, your wife may have had a stroke, or she may have had some form of aneurysm, third she potentially could have a brain tumor. We won't know until she gets an MRI."

What? .... What ?... We just got out of a long term, 8 year battle with Leukemia and just as we were feeling like we could experience a real life we have this going on? My mind was racing, trying to grasp what was happening to our family. The whole tunnel phase of thinking began happening all over again, just like the day of Kevin's diagnosis. But this time I didn't have my partner working beside me. She was melting from the inside as her soul was being crushed by this devastating news. Then the doctor says, "Please wait in the waiting room and I will get you set up with an MRI."

I cannot remember if someone came to pick her up, or if she remained in the waiting room. I don't think I will ever know unless I go through hypnosis to pull that blocked memory out of my head. I do know that the receptionist called me up to the window and said "The doctor has made an appointment for your wife to have an appointment in two weeks. Here is your scheduled time and location of that MRI Mr. McKeown." I stepped away silently from the window as there was someone waiting behind me, that I do remember. Two weeks, seriously? This is complete B.S. This is a small town in Maine. She deserves better than this. This may not be of importance to them, but to us, well I am not going to tolerate this. That voice in my head said, "Stand up and do something about this. Do not walk out that office door."

So I turned around and waited behind the person at the window. When that person moved back to the waiting room, I approached the receptionist. "Hi, I am Marguerite's husband, we just spoke about her MRI appointment."

"Yes," she said, "what can I do for you?" I leaned towards her the best I could with a chest high counter space and I said quietly and calmly, "You are going to have to call the police please"

"Why" she asked while looking around the waiting room with a curious panicked look on her face.

"Because I am not leaving this office until that doctor gets her an appointment today for an MRI. I will call the local news affiliates, and this is going to be an epic human-interest story for this town as they haul me out of this office in handcuffs" I responded calmly.

She stood up and disappeared, and moments later the doctor appeared from the back of the office area. He was curt and a bit annoyed when he addressed me. "Mr. McKeown, you want the police here, what is the problem?"

I calmly defended my case, but moreover I defended my wife, her honor as a mother and the time that she endured battling cancer. "Well doc, for the past eight years we have been fighting leukemia with our first-born son. Three years of chemotherapy followed by five years of waiting to see if it came back. We received a clean bill of health from Maine Children's Cancer Program roughly two weeks ago. Do you have any idea of what it is like to wait five years to see if your first born has beaten Leukemia? Now you are asking her to wait two weeks before she finds out if she has a brain tumor. We are not new to this office. We have been coming here since we started this family, you yourself have performed eye exams on our son. Now unless you want to explain to the press how you blindly expect us to wait for the news of the MRI results, I am asking that you pull some strings. Find a hospital that can do this. I will drive her to Boston if I have to, but she will know tonight before she puts her head on her pillow. She deserves at least that." I said as though it were a script that I memorized from a screenplay. I stared at him as if to say, go ahead tell me there is nothing you can do, I dare you.

"Alright, let me see what I can do," he said as he bowed his head and walked away. I returned to the lobby, unable to sit. I paced with wild staring eyes of someone that had desperation written all over my face. Some time elapsed and he returned to the lobby area with a slip of paper. Here is an address and a time. I am sorry and I did the best I could. Good luck," and he lowered his head and walked away. I glanced at the paper. It was an intown address with a set time of nine p.m. I left with a sense of accomplishment. Yet knowing this was only going to be a small piece to this obviously. I was hoping for the mildest of things. But which of the three possibilities would be mild?

We went to the address at 9:00 p.m. that night. There was a technician there that unlocked the door for us. He confirmed her identity and brought her to the exam room where the MRI was located. I waited in the hallway alone. There was no one there. The eye doctor must have called in a big favor for this one. The image was taken, and the results were sent to a doctor who was at home. The results were not only made but the technician placed the call on a speaker phone for us to listen to in the lobby at the reception desk. The results, it is a brain tumor. Located almost in the center of the brain, and it appears to be self-encased, but still, it is a brain tumor.

Marguerite collapsed in my arms, crying and sobbing so hard. She was obviously petrified and all I could do was hold her. Was I proud of the results of finding out before her head touched her bed pillow? No, not at all, but we could move on from this point. The anguish of waiting two weeks when this mother of three waited five years to see if her son was cured. Well simple as rain, she didn't deserve that. She deserved a lot better. I had to figure out what the next plan was, but first it was time to take her home.

It was after midnight when she called a friend – the one person that she could confide in and that would come over. It was the neighbor who wouldn't let her kids play with ours. Their friendship had grown and Marguerite was really depending on her. Sure enough, that neighbor came over and was supportive for an hour or so until we realized that we all should get some sleep. The problem will be there in the morning, so sleep was most important in order to face this head on.

The next morning, I called out of work, as did she, and I looked for a neurosurgeon knowing that perhaps the small town that we lived in didn't have the state's best residency at their hospital. I went to Scarborough and found reviews on a doctor. I made a call and pleaded for an urgent appointment. It was within a few days that we were booked to see this leading surgeon. He viewed the MRI and said that he felt very confident that it was self-encased, benign, and had been a slow growing tumor, based on his experience. We were welcomed to go anywhere else for a second opinion, and Boston Hospital had some of the best brain surgeons on the eastern seaboard. We went there in the beginning of October for that second opinion.

Boston read the MRI and they too said it was self-encased. They were as confident as our doctor in Scarborough Maine that it was non-cancerous and slow growing. We should consider having the surgery in Maine so that if there were follow up appointments it would not be difficult to attend. So, we decided to move forward asap and scheduled the surgery for late October. They were going to remove part of her skull on the right side of her head and go in between the two lobes of the brain, the frontal and temporal lobe, until they arrived at the tumor. The surgeon assured that although it was a difficult surgery because it dealt with the brain, that we would be able to move on with our lives once this was done. That was reassuring considering she had a tumor growing in her brain that took away eyesight that she wasn't aware of.

Well, we had some loving friends of hers meet us there at Maine Medical Center. It was early, but they were there nonetheless. The nurses prepared Marguerite for the surgery by gathering her clothing, providing a Johnny or two, and starting an IV. Ten minutes before it was time, they gave her something to calm her down, take the edge off. She immediately calmed down

It was that morning that she told me her wish. She said I want you to find someone to love if I don't make it. You deserve someone. I said I have someone, and you are not going anywhere. If only they offered the spouse something to calm them down too.

I held her hand until they took her away through the double doors of surgery with signs that read *Authorized Personnel Only*. I retreated to a bench that was in this long dark cold hallway and I lost my composure. I sobbed and cried as though there was no hope. I could not hold back. I had tears falling like rain, mucus draining from my nose. I was a hot mess and felt the end of my world was coming.

"We've got to get going," I heard a voice say. "Let us know how it goes, we are praying for you." I raised my head and watched the support team walk away.

Why should they stay, I thought, Marguerite has gone into surgery and there is nothing they can do for me. However, it took a few years of telling other people my story and hearing, no one stayed with you? No one from her family, brothers, sister in law were there. I had family that were local too. I sat alone knowing that I had to wait at least 6 to 8 hours for her to come out of surgery. Our sons were being cared for through a prearranged sitter. What was I supposed to do with my time now? I never planned that part out. All I wanted to do was make sure she was well cared for. I second-guessed how pathetic I must have looked after they took her. What else would anyone do but walk away, in order to remove themselves from that situation. I went to the cafeteria and drank my share of coffee, I walked around, I drove around Portland and South Portland in a haze. Did a little tour around Cape Elizabeth and found myself sitting back in the parking lot of the hospital. I had not eaten since the day before, coffee in the cafeteria was the only liquid intake I had, yet I was not thirsty nor hungry. I was consumed with thoughts of what was happening. Were they paging me to explain the success or the failure of the surgery?

I went back into the hospital and wandered down to the surgery ward. Surprised I could find my way, actually. A labyrinth of halls and double doors that might fit in a Steven

King movie. I spotted a nurse who seemed to be working in the area so I inquired about my wife who was undergoing brain surgery under the care of Dr. Barth. Yes, let me check on her for you. She disappeared behind a pair of double doors, then returned to tell me she was in post op and that I could see her if I wished. "Yes, please," was all I could manage to say. She led me to the post operating room and recovery area. Marguerite was lying on her back with her head bandaged. Handrails up, IV's and monitors still attached and functioning. I approached her and saw her blink a few times.

"Hey sweetheart, how are you feeling"? I gently whispered. She acknowledged me with a whisper saying she felt okay, but had a hard time seeing. Then she sat up and violently vomited. Where did that come from, and what was she vomiting? This poor girl hadn't eaten in probably 26 hours. She moaned and the nurse said that I should probably go. I reached out to hold Marguerite's hand and said that I would wait outside in the hallway. Some time went by and a nurse passed by to tell me they brought her up to her room. I was disappointed to find out that she had been moved and I hadn't even seen her pass by. Obviously, a different route for patient transporting which is something I wasn't aware of until later. I found her in her room, half sleeping, half coherent. She had been through a lot and I still didn't know what that whole violent vomiting episode was about. Yet she seemed peaceful enough. The nurse explained that she needed her rest and that I should return home to catch up on my own. She was right and I had a lot of phone calls to make, plus check in on the boys.

The next morning, I was at the hospital before sunrise and in her room to greet her as she woke up. Still groggy and more upset that she now couldn't see very well out of either eye. I tried reassuring her that it was less than 12 hours ago that she's come out of surgery, and that recovery was going to be part of her stay. She continued to fall in and out of sleep and I had yet to have a coffee. Far too excited to see her and get an update. I whispered to her that I was going to get coffee and that I would be right back. She shook her head in millimeters and I retreated from the room.

A purchase of coffee and right back to her room only to find an empty bed. A bathroom break certainly wasn't possible. I looked around to ask for help in locating her and I finally spotted her nurse

"Hey, where is Marguerite?" I asked.

"Dr. Barth was looking for you. He had to take her back to surgery, he didn't have time to wait for you, so he had Marguerite sign the permission form. She is back in surgery right now."

What a Twilight Zone moment I was experiencing.

*Something is going terribly wrong with my wife; I went to the cafeteria to grab a quick coffee and scoot back to her room only to find out all this has taken place. Why was she required to go back? What in the world is going on?*

I never felt so alone and confused as I did at that moment. Despair filled my heart and my anxiety level was confusing my thinking and judgment. I went to the elevator to head down and find Dr. Barth. I pushed the button and an elevator was coming up to meet my request. When the elevator door opened, there was Dr. Barth with a clipboard. "Oh there you are, I was just coming up to see if I could find you," he said. Simple and matter of fact, as though he was in the area and just stopped by to see if I wanted to go have lunch or something.

"What is going on? She has to go back into surgery, like an emergency? What happened?" I impatiently inquired.

"She had a bleed and it filled the area where the tumor was. We don't know the cause of it, so we are going back in to take a look around. It shouldn't take long, she went through all the hard stuff yesterday. Just a few hours and we will send her right back to you. It's all going to be okay." he responded with the greatest of confidence.

A courtroom defense attorney could not have played a more convincing argument of how his client is innocent of the charges, and yet I felt hollowed out like a cheap chocolate Easter bunny. Numb of thought as well as emotion. Still another day alone facing the potential loss of my best friend. What was going on with us?

At some point I began wondering if this was some modern-day biblical test. We had experienced enough self-doubt and 'why me' complexities to fill a lifetime when our son Kevin was fighting Leukemia. Why me lord? What did I do to deserve this lord? Am I being punished for something in my life that I did?

If you ever have to experience the heartache of a difficult life struggle, or have already, then hear these words. Read them aloud so you can reflect on what is being read aloud. *God has nothing to do with any of this. You have nothing to do with any of this. If you want to place blame on something, or someone, then put it where it will be used properly. This is the work of evil. Satan if you want, demons if that better suits you.*

A TASTE OF HOPE

There are opposites for everything in the universe. Light and darkness, hot and cold, happy and sad. The infinite list at this point is self explanatory. Why wouldn't there be an opposite of good. Something opposite of God like. A force that is deceptive, powerful and lies to manipulate what it wants above what is right and good.

This is the one thing that I used to my advantage to stay true to myself and to my faith. Who is full of lies? Satan. Who is deceptive, cunning and looking to destroy the faith of mankind? Satan. Who would rejoice in being so devious that he has made you think and believe that it was God's will that you must undergo these difficult trials? Satan. Now tell me this; what would defeat him in his quest? Where can you muster the strength from within, like sunshine to Superman? Make the recipe for the taste of hope yourself.

Take a moment for yourself to regroup. Sit down on a bench, even if it is in the busiest of places. Close your eyes and slowly take in a breath of air, filling your lungs. Feel them expanding. Hold it, then let it out slowly through your nostrils and repeat two more times. While you are doing this and thinking only of your breath, realize that there is no good or bad in the world, but thinking makes it so. Now take the blame or pity from your heart where it was pointing at you and or God. Now use your energy to spread love, to be grateful for the positive things. Make Satan regret that you got out of bed this morning. Make this journey of yours important enough that God himself smiles at your tenacity, dedication, strength.

Be as unyieldingly brave as Gandalf on the bridge of Khazad-dum as he defied Balrog from passing in the Lord of the Rings.

I believe that the deception of evil comes in many shapes and sizes. It is easy to enter into anyone's heart and mind if it is weak and vulnerable enough. Stay strong in the hours of doubt. Know that you are not alone, but the demolition of your spirit is the prize that Satan wants. To make you think that God has abandoned you in your darkest hours. He may even whisper in your ear that Jesus had the same feeling of abandonment while he was on the cross. Typical isn't it? A thought that makes you a comparison to the son of God, that you were abandoned just like him? Well I have news for anyone who has that moment of doubt and speculation of their purpose and life journey.

YOU'VE GOT THIS! Pick yourself up, and be that dedicated, loving, caring person that you know you can be. Be true to it. Feel the presence of joy begin to fill you. Feel the strength that comes from your core. Your spirit which feels a fire like you have not felt before.

Now compare that to what you were thinking thirty or forty minutes before. Which feels better? See, there is no bad or good – but thinking makes it so. When we feel as though we are beaten, what is it that brings on that emotion? Fear of the unknown? Change perhaps. Possibly a change that we do not want to experience and one that will give you a different outlook on life, if not a completely different track of life all together. Change is important. We must live with change and cope with it daily.

Most of those educational teachings are easily overlooked. When we look at weather, for example, we realize that it changes all the time. Do we still lay on the beach when the rain begins because we refuse to deal with the change? Certainly not. In fact, you won't prove a point to anyone who is watching you. So be accepting of change and expect that change will happen when you least expect it. Your life will be shorter if you fight change. It will build anxiety and stress in your soul, and your life. Accept the rainy day off at the beach and take in a movie instead. You might be surprised what happens.

What about me? What happened? I spent another day aimlessly, not knowing what to do with myself. I was experiencing the deepest of despair. Was I being taunted by evil? Who can say, really?

Marguerite went into surgery at 7 a.m. Now it was 1:00 p.m. and she still wasn't out. I was becoming more than worried. At around 4 p.m. I had decided to walk out to my vehicle again. As I walked across the parking lot I stopped. Right in the middle of the parking lot roadway I looked up towards the clouds over me and yelled at the top of my lungs, "I just want to grow old with her – is that too much to ask!!!?" It was at that moment I realized I'd done it out loud. Oh no, I thought. Is this an empty parking lot? Nope. On the contrary there were several people, all who stopped dead in their tracks and were staring right at me. I put my head down and shook it no. I focused on the pavement only until I arrived at the vehicle, unlocked the door and sat inside silently. It felt like hours had passed but it was only about twenty five minutes or so. Restlessly I returned to the hospital surgery area. There, after 12 hours, they told me that she was in recovery. Dr. Barth would see me tomorrow, but he found nothing that would have caused the bleeding. She was fine and would be brought up to intensive care, where she would stay for a couple days.

This journey was coming to a conclusion. She was soon to find out that she would lose her Peripheral vision just beyond center in each eye. It would affect her depth perception, reading ability, and if it were not to come back in six months then it probably wouldn't come back at all. I was heartbroken for her, yet it appears that my shoutout desire in the parking lot was understood. I could take her home and grow old with her.

CHAPTER

# 7

## SO YOU THOUGHT YOU WERE DONE?

There are daily details that exist in this memoir which I will probably regret because I failed to mention it until after this book is in print. I did not keep a journal of my ordeal but instead I chose to write from my memory and my heart. As my favorite mentor Eckhart Tolle mentions, the ego of ourselves is always seeking attention and desires drama. I have no interest in that whatsoever. I can attest that Marguerite and I wanted only to live a life of fun, goal setting to better ourselves as well as provide our sons the best opportunities that we could muster from our financial means and our own capabilities. After all, if I were a rocket scientist or a famous actor there would be more opportunities and connections for them just because of who I was, in the limelight of society.

Marguerite and I knew each other's fears and breaking points. Yet we managed to come out on top of these past nine years with sanity at the helm. We had no drug addictions, alcohol dependencies, nor did we have such a turbulent relationship that we were on the brink of divorce. Not at all. We realized what our strengths and weaknesses were and supported one another when we would have a weak or dark moment. So fighting childhood Leukemia and now her brain tumor were challenges we met together. However, I admired her bravery. She was a locomotive when it came to wanting to be there for the boys and me. She knew she had me as her best friend and soulmate in life, and that I would do anything to keep her safe and happy. That comes in a lot of shapes and sizes. It varies from picking up my socks and underwear off the floor to protecting her at a concert when the crowd starts to get rowdy. I speak with pride and wonderment of her mothering skills and devotion to our boys.

She also knew when to brag about me in certain circles as an involved dad or hard-working husband that provided for her and the boys. She never labeled me in a negative light, and any failures that I had experienced were forgiven and kept within the privacy of our home. I treat her the same way. We did not complain behind each other's backs to our friends or coworkers. That is petty and juvenile, not the ingredients for a great marriage.

She was first on my list of priorities in my life, then the boys. She is independent of me as well as a part of me. The experiences of fighting childhood leukemia with our son while raising one other then our third during the third year of treatment was terrifying. I seldom told her of my fears and thoughts as I tried staying strong for her. It turns out that she was doing the same for me and the boys. Keeping that strong face 98% of the time. We had our moments, but for me most of my breakdowns occurred at work while I was hiding behind a full face respirator spray painting. I had experienced a few breakdowns like this. Sometimes driving in the car alone and having to pull over just to let the sobbing, heartfelt cry loose and to get it out of my system. It always felt better.

It was after her surgery and six weeks of daily radiation to kill the remaining remnants of the tumor that was growing from her optic chiasm. We were going on a date. Just her and I going shopping, being together while we toured Portland Maine as well as South Portland, where we would go to the mall and simply enjoy the day together. We were driving home on the turnpike north towards our hometown and as we approached a straight away section where there was a small clearing without trees. That is rare on the turnpike because Maine is heavily forested. There was a massive tree at the northern portion of this clearing that we drove by hundreds of times. As we approached it she began telling me one of her deepest secrets that she had been holding onto.

"You see that big tree at the end of the clearing up ahead?" she asked. My heart began to race, and my breath was shortening. "Yeah," I said.

"Well, there were times during Kevin's treatment when I was driving home from the hospital alone that I thought about driving into that tree." She gazed at me with anticipation of what I would say as I drove past it. I began a slow, monotone, muffled scream with my hand covering my mouth in the car.

"What? What's the matter? I would never do it with the kids in the car, it was just…" I raised my hand to stop her from speaking anymore. I paused, swallowed and softly uttered these words. "That was my tree too. I often thought of the same fate with that very same tree."

The car ride was silent for a while. I think we both grew a deeper respect for one another. We were both experiencing the same depths of pain, but we had strength from our marriage, our faith in God which was restored after faith sharing and counseling.

I want to enlighten those of you who have moments of doubt that you could continue to go on. There are people out there who have experienced far worse than Marguerite and I have. Thinking about taking your own life I believe is a natural human thing and at some point, in someone's life they will think about it. It is depicted in books, movies, and the Bible. Even the movie *It's a Wonderful Life* has the entire theme wrapped up in the imagination of 'what if I never existed, what if I ended my life.' I am worth more dead than alive, said Jimmy Stewart.

What is crucial about thinking this is that it stops there. Our thought processes go to great lengths in imagining things. But what we cannot do is make a plan to execute. Yes, it is hypocritical of me to say that when we both had a tree picked out to drive into right? However, I never wrote a note saying goodbye, I never made accommodations for my family to be cared for. I also never chose a day and a time. It was a passing thought for me as I drove by the tree. Was it a demon's influence? Preying on a weak moment to break my will to survive this?

I will let you decide how you view the world of influencers and demons. Some may think we are alone in the immense galaxy, while others may feel that we are descendants of aliens that were deposited here. I do not claim to have any answers to this, nor am I suggesting anyone is right or wrong. What is important here is that you find in your mind what works for you. What positive influences make you a better person or what influences bring you down a path of negative results, or worse the path of self-destruction. Play that fight song, eat that comfort food or do the thing that is harmless but gives you pleasure and happiness. Now that you are in a different frame of mind, make a better plan. A stronger plan with a single goal. What is your taste of HOPE? What flavor can you imagine it will render you? Allow your concentration to be focused on that, and not the negative voice in your head.

So that was the end of our story, all our troubles are behind us right? Marguerite and I worked diligently to rise above our setbacks. She decided to finish her college degree. She dropped out when she was younger, before we both met. She was prompted by coworkers to go back and finish her degree. So with apprehension she enrolled in the University of Southern Maine where she went to complete her degree in Social and Behavioral Science. It was one year in that she decided to double major, and in time she graduated from USM with her degree Social and Behavioral Science with a minor in education. Our three sons and I were in attendance on that glorious day. She graduated with so much more than just a degree. She had progressed through some of the most difficult and challenging moments in life. The degree was to me a victory for her past 13 to 14 years of winning over a foreboding cloud of doom. To this day I am so proud of her for completing it and striving never to give up.

I realized in 1998 that I wanted to begin a college pursuit, however I wasn't sure of what. It was after some soul searching that occupational health and safety came to mind. We both wanted to accomplish something new and positive in our lives as well as setting a positive example to our sons that we should never stop learning and self improving.

Time passed as our boys were growing into their teen years. We wanted to provide opportunities to them. 'You will never know if you like something until you try it.' Football, hockey, soccer, basketball, baseball, music, art lessons, Boy Scouts, biking, tennis, hiking. We couldn't afford skiing, but we tried ice skating as often as we could. Volunteering for the local hospital as young teens was also a positive influence. Altar boys at our local Catholic church. All of this and good parenting were what we thought was needed for well-rounded young adults coming into the world.

Yes, there was down time and their own interests such as Pokémon and Marvel comics. Video games that were only allowed for a half hour per boy if their homework was done. Once the half hour was up, they either shut it off or passed it to a brother. Reading, going outdoors or something other than a video game was required.

When it came to Boy Scouts, I wanted them to have a similar experience to what I had. When I grew up as a young man, first in Rhode Island then moving to Maine when I was 15, I wanted to finish my pursuit of becoming an Eagle Scout. I made it, just under the wire, but I made it and with that some of the best moments of growth as a young man that I could have never received from simply remaining in school. All three of our sons also completed their Eagle Rank which

I hope is something that will be cherished for them as much as it is for me.

See, life can convert back to a sense of normalcy. So if you are experiencing something life changing and wondering what a "Normal life" looks like, just know this. Normal is really only a setting on your clothes dryer. There is no set standard of normal. It is what you make it. We pursued our dreams of what that would look like for us.

I ask you this, are we confusing normal with average? What does the average American family do when they are raising kids? How do we fit into the description of the all American family? There is no defined criteria for that. We as a human race have the ability to do what we wish and unfortunately society places judgment on what the collective community sees as normal. I am not attacking that as much as I am attempting to reach out to those who are chasing something just so that they can feel like they fit in. The social peer pressure of "you've gotta do this."

If you are down and lost due to a life challenge, just let it take its course. You may be in a funk for longer than you thought, but as long as you hold on and continue each day doing the best you can, you will get through what you are going through. So by now you are thinking to yourself, this author has gone through a couple of rough patches and survived, good for him and his family. Right? Well we really don't know what is in store for us when the sun rises over the horizon each morning.

It was in 2002 when a third catastrophe hit our family. It was a nightmare of bizarre proportions that had me doubting the difference between reality and what Hollywood portrays as fictional horror. It began with us bringing our boys to the circus in Portland. Ringling Bros. and Barnum & Bailey Circus was in town. We had been to a circus before, but this could be perhaps the last time that we decided to go as a family since the two older boys would grow out of this.

However, they did not contest that they had no interest or refused to go. Our son Brian was hanging around with a new friend he met so we called and asked if he would be interested in going. His mother who answered the phone asked and he said sure, he would go with our family. I drove to their house with the family in tow and once we got to the highway and began our journey to Portland it was becoming clear that Brian's friend was not just sick with a cold, but this young man should have stayed home. Turn around and take him home, be late for the show, or take him thinking perhaps we are making more of this than we should.

This was a Saturday afternoon during a winter weekend in February. We had a decent time regardless of the coughing and hacking from this young man. We did not make any new plans like pizza or ice cream stops on the way home. Instead, it was a a mission to get him home to rest. He was exhausted on the way home. No doubt he was feeling worse than when we picked him up. We have all seen it. That flu that creeps up on you and then within a couple hours you begin to wonder what is happening. Chills, body aches, a nagging pain in your chest and when you cough, well it feels like you are breaking off a piece of lung it hurts so bad. We dropped him off and went home.

The next day we hadn't seen much of Brian. He was staying away from not only us, but his brothers as well.

Marguerite asked Shawn where Brian was, and he said he was in his room listening to music. Music was a newfound passion for Brian, so listening to it was perfectly fine with us. Brian's personality has always been that of the sweetest and loving personalities you would have the pleasure to mee, but that Sunday, there was something wrong.

Marguerite wanted to talk to him so she called for him. "Brian, come upstairs and see your mommy, I want to ask you something" she called to him from our upstairs addition. Brian finally came upstairs into the living room which was over our two-car garage.

He said sharply "What?!" Marguerite and I were both taken back by this sharp sassy attitude.

I recall looking at him saying "Uhmm excuse me, do not talk to your mother like that." He merely glanced at me with darting eyes. That struck me as odd–something was wrong. He was upset, but why? His brothers maybe? Teasing and fights between brothers are a part of any family.

"Brian, come see me," said Marguerite.

"NO! You want to say something, say it from there, I can hear you just fine," stated Brian defiantly.

I did not spring to my feet, which is something I was on the brink of doing, but I could feel the heat rush over my face and my heart began to beat twice its speed. "This is not an acceptable attitude or way to talk to your mother or me," I told him.

"So?" he replied.

"Brian, go to your room right now. You stay there until you are called, is that understood?" said Marguerite.

He stood there staring at her. His gaze was intense. He wasn't moving.

"Did you hear your mother?" I asked him. His head pivoted to glare at me, stared intensely at me then back at her.

"I hate you!" he proclaimed. I sprang up to my feet and he stepped back but stood glaring at me as if to say, go ahead, come at me. I advanced and he retreated to his room. I followed and explained to him he was to stay there until dinner.

"I don't care about dinner; I hate you too," Brian snapped back. I went back upstairs to talk to Marguerite and I asked as soon as I appeared in the room.

"What the hell was that about?" We sat there bewildered. Thoughts racing in our minds of what could be causing this outburst. Is he having some sort of breakdown or rebellious period where puberty is messing with his hormones? No, this is too weird for that. Could he have been taunted at school and is being bullied? No, probably not. We would have seen something right away after school. Was he molested by someone and is acting out? How could that be a possibility? He is always in our sight with the exception of him going to the bathroom in a public place. Could that have been it? He was molested by someone who saw him as a quiet kid. Oh God no, please not that.

That evening passed and as any concerned parent would do, we checked on Brian to see if he was ready to talk, eat something or have something to drink. Oddly he just wanted to be left alone and was not willing to talk, eat or anything that involved cooperating with his parents. We checked on him at bedtime and he was fast asleep so we left him alone for an uninterrupted night's sleep.

My routine to make it into work usually began at 4 a.m. With the shipyard being roughly 45 minutes away, conducting a search for parking and settling in for a cup of coffee before the day began was a decent and comfortable way to start my workweek. The shipyard had a zero tolerance policy for being late. Work was my bread and butter for my family, and it has done well with providing me with stable income as well as a good medical coverage plan.

So between 5:00 and 5:30 a.m. I was out the door. As I was getting ready to walk out the door Brian emerged from his bedroom. He approached me somberly and said in a mature apologetic voice, "Dad, I am really sorry for yesterday."

"Brian, thank you for saying that, you didn't have to get up to tell me that. What happened yesterday? What were you upset with?" I inquired.

He said he wasn't sure but was really sorry and that he felt terrible. We hugged, and I told him that he needed to tell his mother the same thing when she got up. Wished him a happy day at school, asked him not to worry about yesterday and we can talk about it tomorrow.

That day when I arrived home, Marguerite met me at the door. She said the middle school called her at work and said there was something wrong with Brian. He sat in class when he was dismissed to go to his music class. His music class was his very favorite class of all. The teacher said he simply sat there, staring at the board, non-responsive to comments or questions by the teacher. Marguerite took him home and he only wanted to go to bed. Yet Marguerite was distraught. She had seen a side of Brian that she had never seen before.

She said to me, "He thinks I am trying to kill him," as she welled up in tears. I remember looking at her with confusion and disbelief. What? No. He must be playing some weird trick. "Go see for yourself," she said.

I opened Brian's bedroom door. The blinds were drawn closed and the curtains were pulled closed. His bedroom was on the east side of the house and February Maine darkness was making his room very dark.

"Hey Brian, what is going on? How are you feeling?" I softly inquired. A slow but almost baritone voice filled the room with a haunting chill. "Mmmooooooommmmmmm iiiiisssssssss trrrrrrrrrryyyyyyyyiinnnng toooooooo killllllllllllllll meeeeeeeee."

If you are seeking a comparison, then I will refer you to the movie *The Shining* by Stephen King. The little boy Danny who rode his tricycle down the halls. Well, when he was possessed by the spirit Tony, he spoke in a similar voice to Brian's. But Brian's voice scared the hell out of me. I was terrified to be in the room, yet I remained calm on the outside for everyone's sake. "Brian, why would you say that? Your mom loves you. She isn't trying to kill you."

"Shhhhheeeeeeeeee is trrrrrrrrrrryyyyyyyying to pooooiisssssssooonnnn meeeeeeee." I immediately responded with a one-word question,

"How?"

He pointed to the Tupperware vintage 16 oz. orange cup.

"Pooooiiiisssooooooooonnnn!!!" I looked inside and saw it was half filled with water.

"Brian, that is water not poison."

"NO! IT'S ORANGE! ORANGE POISON!" he retaliated with that newly discovered baritone voice. A voice that was not his own, nor the voice that I heard at the beginning of that very same day.

I stepped out of his room and closed his door. Shawn called out to me from his room where he and Kevin were. As I stood in the doorway of his room, he looked at me with deep concern and asked, "Is Brian going to be okay?" I nodded with confidence to them both that he was going to be just fine. Just a flu bug or something I said in confidence, simply hoping that they would buy it. Hoping that my calm demeanor would be enough to feel that everything was okay. In reality I was afraid to go back into his room. Afraid of what I might find. Yes, Hollywood has gotten the best of me at this point. Visions of terrible things were going through my head, and most of it was based on some form of demonic possession. How else do you explain the voice change?

But seriously, STOP thinking that. Be realistic, I continued to reassure myself. When I approached Marguerite, she knew what I heard. "Well?"

"Oh you are absolutely right, there is something wrong. He cannot identify that the water is water. He thinks it is 'orange poison.' I think we are going to have a long night, but he has to go to the hospital. Let's get the boys fed, and hopefully us if we can stomach something, and find someone to watch Kevin and Shawn.

"Ask Brian if he is hungry" she said next.

Reality was a huge confidence booster for me and I stepped back into his room. "Hey Brian, hungry? What would you like for supper?" It was then he rolled over from his facedown position lying on the bed and spoke to the ceiling without making eye contact with me. "I waaaaaannnnnnnttt a chheeeeeessse buuurrrrrggger—and ooooonnnnnnneeeee sssssttttrrriiiiiiiiiinnnnnng beeeeeeean."

This was his request for supper. We were able to get someone to stay with Brian's brothers. We gathered our coats and headed to the hospital. Central Maine Medical Hospital, which is the second largest hospital in the state and luckily right in our hometown. We arrived around 6 p.m. at the emergency room, waited for our names to be called, and within a short amount of time, we were brought out back to an examination room.

He was seen and examined. Our testimony was given, but Brian was not speaking in the baritone voice anymore. Brian simply wasn't talking. He would only stare. A few hours passed and the decision to do a lumbar puncture and test his spinal fluid was next. We had to convince Brian to lay down on his side, curl up in a ball and hold perfectly still. The doctor told us that we had to encourage Brian to hold perfectly still when they were doing the spinal tap. One wrong move would be extremely damaging to Brian's spine. After I failed to convince him the water wasn't poison, what was he going to think or do when we did this?

Once again, I was asked to help keep him calm. Talk to him to prevent sudden movement. Sound familiar? Now I was dealing with a 13-year-old almost as tall as I am, not a two-year-old. Spinal tap instead of breaking into the pelvic bone.

What is it with moments like this when your brain begins to fog? I was involuntarily paralyzed. A natural defense mechanism? I had no thoughts about the world around me, the room I was in, the people that were there. I simply concentrated on keeping him as calm as possible and told him this would be over very quickly. It wasn't something that was going to happen and keep happening for a long period of time.

"Done! Great job, Brian. Great job, Mom and Dad," said the doctor. "I am going to test this and get back to you. Stay here, this shouldn't take long."

So we waited. We waited as though it was as easy as going to a lab and turning around. But we didn't know what was involved. We only knew time was crawling. The singer Gordon Lightfoot sings of the wreck of the Edmund Fitzgerald with lyrics "Does anyone know where the love of God goes when the waves turn the minutes to hours?"

Well, a sinking ship is not the only era of time that is lost. Not when you are fighting for the life of a loved one. A child that you brought into the world, who has trust and confidence that you are going to do right by them. It was past midnight and we hadn't heard anything. Brian was still. Sleeping as comfortably as possible. Finally the doctor returned. He approached us both and said, "You are in very murky dark waters. Brian has a strain of encephalitis and should be treated at Maine Medical Center in Portland."

"How—how is he going to get to Maine Medical Center? Are we taking him?" I inquired.

"No, he is going by ambulance. It is too risky to take him by helicopter," he replied. "I have an ambulance team that is assembling and will be taking him. You can follow them; it shouldn't be a problem."

I spoke with the ambulance driver who said he wasn't going to do anything but drive our son to Maine Med. We both felt a bit of relief, yet the *Taste of Hope* was bland as Tofu. It was way too early to bank on hope yet.

As we assembled behind the ambulance for the 45-minute drive, we were both in shock at what was taking place. We pulled out onto Main St. and began following our son being transported by ambulance. Only one block was traveled when we peered down a side street. It was there, at 1:30 a.m., that we witnessed several teens playing in the street. The girls were on the boys' shoulders. They were without jackets, but fully engaged in the age-old chicken fight or shoulder wars. This was a bitter discovery that the world wasn't fair. We had done everything we could to keep our sons safe, healthy, well fed, educated, loved and raised with the confidence of life. Yet there we were, witnessing several teenagers with no jackets at 1:30 in the morning, in February, in Maine frolicking with no care in the world, nor did their parents know where they were.

I was cut off by a redlight from keeping up with the ambulance. I didn't worry, because the driver said we could follow him. Nothing to worry over. Easy, slow transport. The minute and a half of sitting at the light went by and we continued. However, we realized that we should try to catch up to the ambulance. I drove well beyond the speed limit that early February morning, however I never caught up to the ambulance. Our *Taste of Hope* suddenly turned sour.

CHAPTER

8

# LOW TERRAIN ! PULL UP! PULL UP!

Well, once again we were a family of regular visitors at Maine Medical Center. This time we were visiting the newly renovated Barbra Bush wing and Brian has an entirely new personality that has emerged since his admittance. The deep baritone demonic voice has been replaced with a fairly close imitation of Mario from the Nintendo game *Mario Bros*. He was very comical and did not have a filter regarding what he said.

Amazingly, his case was rare enough that a doctor who was retired was requested to come in and evaluate Brian's condition. Indeed, it was encephalitis, but it was caused by what he described as a flu virus that left his blood stream and nestled in his brain. Thus, causing an infection type swelling of his brain. This all explained his personality shifts as it was based on his frontal lobe swelling. The frontal lobe is where your personality lies and is the area that is affected when alcohol is consumed.

I know we were working towards finding out what it was and how to combat this illness, but I was at my all time low of wondering what was happening in our lives. I had never seen anyone have this many medical challenges in my memory. I didn't know what to think of our situation. However, with total honesty I was beginning to wonder if I had some kind of cosmic curse on my family. Marguerite made damn sure that the boys had a well balanced diet, good rest, and warm clothing. We as a team ensured that they had a balance of all that was good and structured. Steered them away from bad habits, surrounded them with positive people that were not going to do things that would create a negative impact on their lives.

What the hell was going on? I won't try to share a false story of my inner thoughts. I am going to tell you, the reader, what I was troubled with in my thinking. Was it the environment? Was it where we lived and the house was actually seeping something like Radon gas? Uranium from a granite ledge below us? What about the occult? What if there is a world of demons that do the work of evil and try to challenge us to hate and blame God for what is happening to us? After all, we were church-going people. I never made a claim to know everything that takes place on this planet. The occult is something that seems to lurk in the shadows of urban legends and occasionally is portrayed in a movie based on a true story. We've all seen these stories, and it is a discussion to have with those of a similar mindset.

Like many times before, I broke down. Marguerite took me into the bathroom of Brian's private room and I sobbed uncontrollably for several minutes. She held me with a warm embrace that no one else could have offered. Being my best friend, she knew what I felt and the exhaustion that we shared. My honor and love for this woman grew stronger and higher over the next several weeks. When the sobbing stopped, I felt relief. There is something to be said for a good cry. It is not a sign of weakness, but a miracle of reflection and strength. It is a process of letting out stress and anxiety when we are at our weakest point. Perhaps that is why it is associated with being weak, but a good cry helps fortify the soul. I felt rejuvenated and was ready to face what we needed to do in order to make him well, and bring him home.

Three weeks Brian remained in the hospital. We, like many times previously, adapted to what was taking place and disrupting what we felt was normal. NORMAL. How often we said that we couldn't wait for things to get back to normal. That to me is a social cliché. It was around that time that life began changing for me. Not how I lived it, but how I viewed it. I will elaborate more on that later, but for now I would like to conclude this life challenge of Brian's before shifting gears to get more philosophical.

After the three weeks passed, it was clear that Brian was out of the woods. He could go home and return to most of his daily tasks and joys. However there were instructions that he should be careful of falling and striking his head. Through his teen and college years he'd have to make sure to stay away from alcohol, as it would take years for his brain to complete its recovery process. In addition to that he was expected to attend

6 months of rehabilitation visits to challenge him with tasks and ensure that the neurons in his brain were reconnecting. When the brain swells like his did, the micron nerves are slowly crushed or pinched in the swelling. That made perfect sense to Marguerite and me. We had to be patient and ensure that he performed all his tasks as we monitored the recovery.

It was a year almost to the day, when Brian experienced a relapse. We couldn't believe it was happening again, and we were petrified of what a second bout of this could do to him. The neurologist assured us that this was not a rare occurrence. It does happen, and it frequently happens on or around the anniversary of the first occurrence. Another spinal tap was needed to perform the test for confirmation. I hated the thought of another invasive procedure that came with great risks if something went wrong. Although it was certainly not as painful as a bone marrow sample.

Confirmation was quick, it was a second round of encephalitis. A prescription of antibiotics and rest were what was recommended. Brian came home and over the next couple of days his condition did not improve, but worsened. We called the doctor who said there was nothing he could do, that we had to be patient. This round of behavior was much different. Brian was walking with his head tipped back at the ceiling. If he wasn't walking through the house like that he was laying down. There were definitely different signs here. His personality was his own, but it was simply the bizarre posture and complaints of a bad headache that he demonstrated.

One of the other side effects was Brian's temper. He was angry and borderline aggressive. I think the one thing that held him back from acts of violence was the pain he was experiencing. Sudden movements made his ache worse. This was a clear indication of a pain threshold and how much someone can take. I think if the situation was different, where he was older and the medical knowledge wasn't available, he would have considered ending his life due to the pain he was experiencing. Everything he said was out of disgust, anger and rage.

Marguerite and I decided to contact her cousin. He was a neurologist and had conducted many operations on the brain as well as other complex procedures. I contacted him and asked what his thoughts were. He asked me to describe Brian's symptoms. After a few minutes of questions, he told me simply to contact Brian's doctor and tell him that Brian needed a "blood patch." He said the doctor would know exactly what that is and what it means. Her cousin continued to explain to me that when the spinal tap/lumbar puncture occurred, most always the opening that was created in the cerebral barrier did not actually close. It is always leaking spinal fluid into his body. His brain realizes it needs to produce more, but it cannot produce enough. The fluid around his brain acts as a cushion and without it, the person, in this case Brian, is experiencing a headache so severe that it makes a migraine seem minimal. It only feels better when he lies down because the spinal fluid is distributing more around his brain.

The *Taste of Hope* was that of honey mellowed by a sweet strawberry. It all seemed so easy and positive. Hope was filling my heart and mind and I had to pursue it until the end.

I called the doctor's office and requested he contact me immediately. I told him that I thought that Brian needed a "blood patch" and without hesitation he said, "How do you know about that?"

"Research," I simply responded. "Will it help?"

His only reply was, "Get him down here as soon as possible." I struck gold. Zero hesitation and an immediate response to make things right as soon as possible was a light of confidence that I needed. I told Marguerite to get her coat and explained to Brian that we had to drive to Portland.

The 45-minute drive to Portland was quiet, and as swift as I could make it without getting a ticket. I explained to Brian and Marguerite the procedure that was going to take place. We arrived at the doctor's office and were brought directly into the treatment room. We were familiar with the plan. The doctor was going to take blood from Brian's arm. He was going to inject the needle and disperse it right in front of the spinal membrane. The blood would create an immediate clot and dam up the leak of his spinal fluid. Once his body produced enough spinal fluid to cushion the brain, he would be pain free.

The doctor drew blood from Brian's arm. Then stepped to the opposite side of the exam table. Brian was upset with me. Probably for taking him from his bed and putting him through this was all I could figure. He stared into my eyes with such hate and discontent.

"I just want to punch you in the face," he told me with such anger and rage.

"Okay," I said. "I tell you what, not yet. But when this is over, you can. How's that?" I bartered.

The doctor told Brian to bend over while sitting up, and I asked if he could lay on his side. The doctor said this position was more effective. Marguerite and I beckoned and begged Brian not to move.

Brian balled up his fist, becoming more upset by the second. I thought he was going to lose it and begin swinging at me. Regardless of that he had a needle in his back millimeters away from his spine.

"DONE!" exclaimed the doctor, who was, I think, five times more nervous than we were. He instructed Brian to lay down on the table and rest. He would return in a few minutes. It was like a Disney movie where a spell was losing its hold on the main character. We watched Brian's sweet and kind personality return as the minutes passed. He drank some water, and when the doctor returned to the room, he too saw the difference. It was a moment of joy and relief that this young man was relieved of his pain and ailment.

As Brian was putting his shirt back on, I told him simply, "Okay you can punch me now if you still want to." He smiled with a hint of embarrassment and shook his head no. We offered to take him to dinner, get something to drink, but all he wanted to do was go home and rest.

It was a quiet ride home with only the radio playing. The three of us were silent. Overwhelmed perhaps, internally rejoicing that within ten minutes of doing a procedure this would be over without damage. As normal as the setting on the dryer would our lives be for a duration that is really unknown. I basked in the *Taste of Hope* that we experienced and could continue to experience.

Arriving home, watching Brian interact with Kevin and Shawn, laughing, feeling relief was the most heartwarming and immediately satisfying feeling. I remember hugging

Marguerite tightly and saying, "If you squeeze me any tighter, I am going to be behind you."

She laughed a hearty laugh. That was the lottery. It had always been like winning the lottery, when we have overcome Kevin's Leukemia, her brain tumor, Brian's encephalitis with this weird complication.

What do I attribute it to? A simple concept or belief system. Never Give Up. We agreed to back each other up. Never stop loving one another, never stop trying. Days when we felt we couldn't do it anymore, we simply reached out like a pro wrestler does on TV and tags their partner. We've got each other's back and we can do this, together. That in itself creates a unique *Taste of Hope* that only those who bond and create that fortitude can know what it tastes like. I will tell you this, the flavor never dwindles, but gets better over time. Does it piggyback off of experience? Perhaps. However, the *Taste of Hope* can be immediate where the foundation of experience has to come with age. Wine is the same. It is either grape juice, something bitter as it ferments, or the final stage–a good tasting wine that progressively gets better, much like experience.

Life continued for us. There was no parade, block party, or recognition on the human-interest portion of the news. We simply and humbly continued with our lives, goals, dreams and pursuit of happiness. We took family vacations, participated in Boy Scouts, school sports, other activities, while we both continued trying to make our way in our jobs and careers.

Then came college planning for Kevin, which was very surreal. I was in awe that the little boy who had fought for his life at the age of two would be soon going off to college. We supported his dreams. He wanted to study art. Searching for art schools was a challenge. It was a desire to make his dream come true, but also to keep him close to us. It was a shock when he insisted on going to Japan to study art.

Seriously, what parent hasn't had to reel in one of their children from a thought that is close to impossible without breaking the bank? After all, the only lottery we had won was that of survival, never a monetary win. Kevin settled for a Western New York college, Brian went the following year to New Hampshire College, and eventually Shawn went to Maine University. All three received handsome scholarships for their achievement of reaching the rank of Eagle Scout. Which we probably had already invested in cumulatively through the years of being boy scouts.

So the college years went by. Holidays of homecoming, and sharing with mom and dad only what they want us to know about their college experiences. Let's not kid ourselves. Children are never ever going to share the details of everything that happens in college. It is a rite of passage. It has nothing to do with a specific generation but a need for independence. There are dozens of examples of this in movies such as Animal House or The Graduate. I get it, and for the most part I understand. Our greatest hope is the outcome, besides the experiences. College life should be a great experience, but education is the goal for propelling that individual forward with knowledge they would not have gotten without that degree.

When Shawn was graduating from the University of Southern Maine we had made a few changes in our lives. I was no longer working at the shipyard. Twenty-eight years and a desire to do something different was coursing through my veins. A lay-off was just what I needed to make that decision to go and never look back. Although shipbuilding was a good living for me and my family, there was more to be said for what I could offer. There seems to be a glass ceiling of how you are seen in a role. Your peers may feel that you are not capable when it really comes down to the inner will and fortitude of you, the individual.

A family decision was proposed. Let's pull up the tent stakes and move to Florida. Two of Marguerite's brothers were there, and the west coast of Florida was a growing and booming metropolis compared to Maine. I personally was tired of the cold and the outdoor work. Snow removal, shoveling off the roof after a heavy snow. Florida was a new environment, and I was ready for it. Would I miss Maine? Yes, to some degree. But there were opportunities I felt were better suited for us there than in Maine. So we moved in 2014 and landed in the Tampa Bay area of Florida. Very close to Clearwater. Moving 1600 miles away was not in my family's comfort zone, but the adventure and opportunity was more exciting than anything else.

The *Taste of Hope* was effervescent champagne that tingled with the taste of life at each thought of what was to come. A three day drive in a modern vehicle, I recall thinking what it was like for early settlers moving all of their belongings and family to a western town for a new beginning. It is better to try and fail than not to try at all, was the only thing I had to remind myself. I so hoped I was doing the right thing for me and my family. *Please don't let this Taste of Hope turn to a disgust of mold from a grape that I didn't notice the fuzz on the unseen side.* Please don't let this move be that.

CHAPTER

9

# YOU CANNOT SURVIVE THIS ONE

September 11, 2014 we pulled into our driveway after a three-day journey to our new home. The place where we would begin our appreciation of warmth, new adventures and discoveries. We rode our bikes in the fall and winter without a worry of being cold. I worked for a month on our house before starting to apply for work. We were blessed to find work as I picked up a job within the month of October and Marguerite found a job in the school system.

Kevin and Brian both ventured off to find what they wanted to pursue and we continued making our house into our home through renovations. Eventually both Kevin and Brian moved out, and Shawn came down in April of 2015.

We experienced outdoor concerts, street celebrations where a couple of city blocks are shut down and dozens of vendors as well as bands play music during the evening for a festive celebration of life. The amazing dynamic appeal of the Tampa Bay area, with all there is to enjoy in so many surrounding towns, was almost exhausting. We sometimes felt like we had to go to work to relax from our weekend of outings and celebrations. Certainly the *Taste of Hope* was proving to be as sweet as honey for us and the decision for the most part seemed to be a good one. We did have a few disagreements that led to some difficulties with questioning the move. But that was more mood of the day than actual remorse.

It was in June of 2015 that Marguerite went to see her primary care physician who noticed a small black mole on the shin of her right leg. Marguerite explained that she had it ever since she was in high school. The doctor wanted her to see a dermatologist so she could validate that it was safe. Marguerite went, and a biopsy was done on this tiny mole. Results came back as skin cancer. This was a surprise for sure. It wasn't discolored, growing in size, but nonetheless, the plan was to remove it entirely and carve out a larger portion of subcutaneous skin to ensure they got it all. The procedure was scheduled, and I accompanied her on the day of the mole extraction.

I am not about to disclose who the doctor or practice was that we dealt with. All I will say is that they were referred to us and they were a local reputable dermatologist practice. The extraction was less than pleasant or worry free. As I sat there in the room silently observing I heard the doctor tell the nursing assistant that he felt that the equipment was less than reliable and he felt he was "hacking" the tissue. Roughly an hour elapsed and the doctor sewed a patch of gauze soaked in betadine to her skin tissue. Really? I thought. Don't you have a bandage that you can wrap and keep it clean with, that we can check on and clean it when needed? Sewing it to the perimeter of the skin seemed grossly primitive to me.

We were sent home and her recovery instructions were to keep her leg elevated and rest. That we did. She kept it elevated and I assisted her with anything needed. The next day she was telling me that it hurt, not just on the site, but her whole leg was sore. It ached to stand on. So I brought her back to the doctor's office without an appointment and complained. They looked at it, said it seemed fine, although the nurse couldn't believe that the gauze was sewn to her skin, but was not about to question the doctor and begged us not to say that she felt it was wrong. Pain medication was issued, bed rest was the recommended remedy.

By July 3rd, just three days after the surgery, she could not lower her leg to the floor. I had to bring the computer chair to her bedside and roll her to the bathroom. It was at that moment that I decided that the hospital was the next step. I brought her to the emergency room and she had to be hospitalized.

How severe? She was a few points away from being septic. This is a life-threatening condition that occurs when the body's response to an infection is compromised and the body's immune system releases a lot of chemicals into the bloodstream. The first week she was in the hospital, it was about trying to save her leg from amputation. The second week was to totally defeat the infection so she could be released.

So, what becomes of something like this? The cause and effect of poor medical practices, not only with a sewn-on gauze but sending her home saying there is nothing wrong? Only to fight for her leg and life with a two-week stay in the hospital. I called one of the largest law firms in Florida and was basically told that we don't have a case unless she lost her leg or life. Okay, so accountability is out the window for poor medical practice. We recovered and moved on with our lives. We planned outings and trips and continued enjoying our lives in Florida for the next 3 years.

One April evening on a work weeknight we were enjoying each other's company while relaxing in front of the TV. It was a little after 7 p.m. and I wasn't really interested in what we were watching. So I asked her if she was happy watching this particular show or if there was something else she preferred to watch. There was no response, so I turned to her to see if she had fallen asleep or was simply preoccupied with something and didn't notice I asked a question. When I looked at her, her mouth on the right side was drooping as was her right eye. I knew at that instant that she was having a stroke. A moment flashed by as I wondered how she could be having a stroke at the age of 57. I calmly reached for my phone and called 911.

With all my knowledge and previous experiences I proceeded to tell the operator that my wife was having what I believed to be a stroke. I was calm, I showed attention to detail for every fact I provided as well as answering questions that were asked of me. I knew that if I wasted time with drama or panic I would delay help for her. Plus I needed her to feel comforted that I had everything under control and that it was going to be alright.

An ambulance and a fire truck arrived and before long I had about four to six men giving her all the attention she needed. They were going to transport her to the hospital since the symptoms were still occurring. They took her and I told her that I would meet them there. I had to gather some information that I am sure they would want to know.

A Taste of Hope

Five minutes, tops, of rushing through the house after her departure in the ambulance, I was in my car heading for the hospital too. I called our sons one at a time and informed them of the occurrence. I thought it was the best thing to do. In hindsight I probably shouldn't have. Wait until the dust settles, it is easier on all parties. Here is why: I called a relative of hers too. I won't say to what degree of a relative, but I wanted this person to know as well. The response I received was devastating. "Well, I am just sitting down to dinner right now." My heart sank. Really? You are basing this call on your supper being interrupted? The respect meter for this person was now below 25 percent and falling fast. I hung up and continued driving.

As I continued my journey, I came upon a bit of a roadblock. There was a large truck used for transporting hot asphalt blocking a lane, if not two lanes. As I safely maintained clearance of the truck, I saw an ambulance that was in an accident. Without a moment of thought escaping my head, I said out loud, "Wow—I thought I was having a bad day."

When I arrived at the hospital, I met Marguerite in the emergency room. She was smiling and relieved that she was experiencing a full recovery. She said that she was able to talk again on the way over to the hospital. Just before the ambulance got into an accident. Stunned, I stood there in disbelief that the wreck that I passed was hers and that the one having a so-called 'worse day' was actually her They kept her for overnight surveillance, and we were released the next day. A couple of weeks went by and she went back to work. The pressure of the children in the school and their behavior, along with what she felt was a lack of support for the ones who were uncontrollable, was simply too much. I told her that I would rather see her out of the school system altogether than go through this on a daily basis. She agreed and enjoyed her time away from school life.

After several months passed, our son Kevin told me that he was concerned that there was something going on with Marguerite. Something that looked like dementia. I told him I didn't think it was that, but something more in line with depression. Empty nest, leaving a career after twenty one years, not knowing what to do in this new stage of her life. He respected my opinion but really asked me to watch her and start considering some of the things that were slowly occurring. I did just that. It began to build and worry me as more and more things occurred that I was noticing. Unfortunately his observations were spot on, I just couldn't see the forest for the trees.

In October of 2019 I took her shopping and we had lunch together. It was a beautiful date. I asked her to go for a bike ride on Sunday. We could make a morning of it. Ride a bike trail, stop in a town to have breakfast and then come home to enjoy the afternoon together. She agreed and we set out that morning. Once we arrived at the parking lot, I unloaded our bikes and got everything ready. She mounted her bike as did I mine, and I began to pedal. It wasn't far that we made it across the parking lot when I heard her bike crashing to the pavement. I looked behind me expecting to see her standing while holding a handlebar as though the bike fell from under her when she stopped. But what I saw was her laid out on her back, eyes closed and squinting in pain. I ran to her, asked her what happened then proceeded to go through the checks before getting her up. We sat on a nearby bench together and I gave her plenty of time to compose herself. It wasn't long before I realized that she had amnesia from striking her head so hard. I took her to the hospital and we were seen by an emergency room doctor who confirmed that she had a slight concussion. She would be fine, but there should be some precautions taken for the next few days.

This was the slope down which she began a slow descent. A descent that was on the precipice of what would be a two-year battle with a global pandemic of COVID, but was unknown at the time. Was it depression? A lack of wanting to do things was becoming more and more obvious, with a combination of less engagement in conversation. I was giving her space because the few times I brought up anything she would become defensive, and it was never a positive conversation in the end.

So, I began researching more and more about her symptoms. Besides typical dementia, there were two other dementia related illnesses. Lewy Body Dementia -of this I wasn't convinced. Then there was Frontotemporal Dementia. Neither were positive diagnoses. Her primary care physician said that there was no way she had either of those. I felt differently, so I took her to a neurologist who convinced us that she had vascular dementia, and the best results in fighting that was hyperbaric chamber therapy. Twenty sessions would promote additional vascular growth in the body and brain. His confidence and my willingness to do anything I could to help her was the combination that took me to the reaches of paying the $5000.00 upfront fee, because it wasn't covered under insurance. When it comes to my wife or children, money has no priority over their health and safety. The *Taste of Hope* was like a bold dark coffee. Strong but bitter. Yet the taste would soon turn sour. Seventeen sessions later in the summer of 2019, and no signs of any improvement. My deciding factor was when she completed her 17th one hour session. As we were leaving on that Monday afternoon she turned to the tech and said, "Have a good weekend." My heart sank and my stomach felt heavy. The decision was made immediately to stop the treatment – recover my 3 visits left since the policy was to pay back what you don't use.

Something else was the cause of her dementia, but it certainly wasn't vascular. Profiteering is how I saw it, but my battle was to find out what was happening to Marguerite. Aside from the hyperbaric chamber treatments there were medications that were also prescribed. Those medications created a zombie of a person who slept most of the day away. When she did wake up, she was off balance. She fell 11 times in 9 months. Some gentle falls and some not so gentle. Never a broken bone, but just enough to scare us both.

August of 2020, in the midst of the pandemic, I found a neurologist located in Tampa who was regarded as the top of her field, with plenty of experience. This is the shortened version of my searches and research to find someone that could help me with a diagnosis. Like our son Kevin's ailment, it was more troubling not knowing what we are facing than knowing. Marguerite and I visited this neurologist more than once. The doctor mentioned that what she really needed was a neuropsychologist to perform a psych exam.

These tended to be a bit grueling. Typically a 5 hour test. This test would be an oral exam performed by the doctor, and we were given a referral.

I called the office on a mid-August day and explained that we were referred by the neurologist with the name provided. The response was defeating, to say the least.

"I'm sorry, we are not seeing patients due to COVID." I found that to be ridiculous and positively stupid. But that was only my opinion, based solely on frustration.

I took Marguerite back to her primary care doctor who wanted us to go to a cancer hospital in Tampa called Moffitt. I sensed a disconnect there in the sense that the doctor wasn't researching anything, but thought that might be a better option. I knew and trusted the neurologist's opinion and called again to make an appointment for Marguerite. I received the same response once again. I questioned how they are earning income and expected to stay in business. How is the receptionist on the phone making a paycheck if money isn't being generated by patients?

"Well," she said, "we are seeing patients, but only a few during the day."

"But she won't see Marguerite?"

"That is correct sir," was the answer.

I hung up. I was so frustrated. I am expected to go to work, engage with people on a daily basis with all the necessary precautions. I have in my career ripped asbestos from naval ships. I have worked in lead environments in both removal of lead paint and in the battery reclamation for recycling. A process that has extreme lead contamination issues, with no signs of asbestosis or mesothelioma, nor did I ever suffer from lead poisoning. Now I have a trained person with a doctorate stating that they are not taking patients due to the pandemic. They cannot figure out a simple means of processing someone safely for a test. I thought about it for a couple days then called them back.

I explained, "My wife was referred to their office. Other doctors are seeing patients. I am in desperate need to know what I am facing here. Your options are to set up an appointment, speak to my attorney who will be contacting you soon, or choose how you are going to answer one of your local news affiliates when I report you to them as a human-interest story for refusing a diagnostic test. That is all I want, a diagnostic test. Discuss it with your staff and let me know what your choice is."

She replied, "I'll call you back," and she hung up.

I hated to go that route but I felt lost, hopeless, and because of the pandemic and fear of when or how it spread people were living in daily fear. The phone rang an hour later, and it was the doctor's office. "How does this Friday at noon sound to you?" With great relief and satisfaction I said "It sounds perfect and I appreciate your efforts to make this happen."

I brought Marguerite to this appointment in Tampa. There were no patients in the waiting room. We sat for what seemed like 20 minutes. Hmmm, they must have all the patients in different exam rooms, I thought. Finally we were called in and I rolled Marguerite into the office in her wheelchair since she now cannot walk long distances.

I brought her into the office and assisted with making her comfortable. The doctor said I was not able to stay in the room and recommended I leave the building. Leaving my cell phone number with them, I decided to drive somewhere local. Three blocks away I spotted a nice 100 yard long park, and decided to spend this time there. It was a grueling time alone, but I was experienced in it as I sat for 2 days alone while she had her brain surgery back in '98. I did not share this appointment with anyone. I could not, as it was so troubling to me that even talking about an exam that would confirm what was truly going on with my wife. It would be depressing beyond what I was currently experiencing. We were married for 33 years. Some 23 years after her brain surgery when I was shouting up to the heavens in the hospital parking lot, ALL I WANT TO DO IS GROW OLD WITH HER! That wish was being granted, however it wasn't how either of us envisioned it.

Perhaps a little after 4 p.m. I received a call from the office. The test is done. She is ready to be picked up. When I arrived I tried to read the room of any positive successes that I could find. Nothing.

"How did it go?" I asked the doctor. She said nothing more than that Marguerite did well. *Wow, there is some real hope.* But I realized that she had to analyze the test results. As I was gathering that conclusion in my mind, she then told me that she would send me an email with a confirmation time to talk the next day.

The following day, I received an email with a scheduled time that the office would call me. The phone rang. She briefed the test results with me line item by line item. Then the words were spoken. I believe through these results that she has Frontotemporal Dementia. I felt relieved that I finally knew and crushed that this diagnosis was it. This disease has no treatment or cure. It progresses quickly for some, over a couple of years, and others it lasts 12 to 15 years. But I finally knew and could now concentrate on this specific issue. I read up on the two variations of FTD and realized that she did not have the behavioral variant. She had the progressive aphasia version. It was all making sense to me now.

One more follow-up appointment with the neurologist who provided the referral. The one I trusted would know or recommend what to do with the next steps. We entered the exam room and the doctor asked Marguerite the same routine memory questions. What day is it, what month is it, who is the president, what state are you in, what county are you in. Then the 4 words to remember. Pencil, table, car, book. 3 more minutes of conversation and then the question of what were the 4 words I asked you to remember?

When that was done the doctor told me what I had already known, "Your wife has Frontotemporal Dementia."

I was then handed a trifold brochure on Frontotemporal Dementia and was told to contact them. The doctor reached for the door handle and asked if I had any questions. My brain goes briefly numb of thought when the people I trust disappoint me. It clouds over like a swift fog off the sea. Thoughts are blurred, words don't form. The world also seems to slow down a little. "No, not at this moment," but I was thinking – Seriously, this is what it comes down to–a trifold brochure? Call them? The doctor opened the door and during the departure I heard the words you can make your way to the front desk to check out.

What just happened... I was polite. Did the doctor who gave the exam tell this neurologist what I did to get the appointment? What does a person do when they want medical attention and answers and the professionals don't offer assistance? We attended one more visit to this neurologist and after the the routine questions – what day is it, what month is it, who is the president, what state are you living in, what county is this that you are in, along with a couple others, the doctor turned to me and said "Great job! She is getting better! I will see you next year!" and darted out the door. Why not tell me she was getting younger too? We both knew that the answers were lies. That was the last time I visited that office.

Frontotemporal Dementia comes with a stigma in society. Whether it is the behavioral variant or the progressive aphasia that Marguerite has. Honestly, the first year after diagnosis, I was at my worst. We beat childhood Leukemia together, we made it through a bout of encephalitis with a relapse the following year. A brain tumor, along with surgeries that plagued our family for just another trip to a hospital or specialist. None were as life threatening as the previous.

This is something I was facing alone on a day-to-day basis. I am not of retirement age. I have a job that I really love now. But she needs constant care. I questioned myself about what Marguerite would do if the shoe were on the other foot. What if it were me with FTD? What would she do? Placing me in a nursing home would be the last resort, that I know. We adore one another. She is my best friend and best friends don't walk away.

It was shortly after the diagnosis, which she only knows is dementia. Not this specific version with the outcome that it has.

She asked me as we sat in the living room, "Please don't leave me."

Oh my heart split in two hearing those words. I felt the lump in my throat surface, and I told her with confidence, "I vowed on the altar during our marriage that I would honor you and cherish you for richer and for poorer, in sickness and in health, until death do us part. Now what you don't know is that our marriage comes with an extended warranty so we are locked in forever."

A broad smile came across her face. The smile that lights up a room. The smile that I strive to see at least 5 times a day when I am with her. There are constant reminders in our world that life isn't fair. I couldn't agree more. It hasn't been fair since the beginning of time. It is what we do with the time that we have. We both just turned sixty years old. My goals have been steadfast and true. I must keep her safe, and happy. It is a daily mission and sometimes I feel as though I am not doing such a great job at it. While my sisters tell me differently. They are my life's cheerleaders as their faith in me helps rebuild my spirit when it's down. My work family is a pleasant distraction from my life as I try to stay focused on my tasks. It is there that I also become distracted as I have issues with hired caregivers from time to time. I lost count after 14 over the past 3 years but it is up there somewhere. Some move on for reasons which I support while others must be let go once they exit the house. I strive to protect Marguerite from harsh attitudes or rudeness by someone who is being terminated.

June of 2022 I came down with COVID. I was not hospitalized, but was feeling absolutely terrible. I had a caregiver at the time who did not want to come to the house to care for Marguerite even if I stayed secluded in a bedroom. I honored that with understanding. I don't want someone to

A TASTE OF HOPE

become ill, yet, I have to care for my wife while I have COVID. A week went by. Bathing her, cooking for her, helping her throughout the house. I thought for sure it was going to be the end of her. Yet I continued my safety practices of hand washing, wearing a mask in my house and maintaining 6 feet away from her when I was not giving her aid. I am proud to say that over the past 3 years since the outbreak of COVID, and the doctors appointments, dinners out, in order to get her out into a fresh air environment, she has never contracted COVID.

What is next you might ask? Well I can safely say at this time we have a fantastic caregiver, Debbie. Though I know that everything is subject to change. She may be offered something new or find a career that pays more than I can afford. We truly love having her with us, however I must be prepared for the things that are outside of my circle of control.

I continue getting up at 3:30 in the morning to start my day. I strive to roll with changes and accept them as they occur because many things are beyond my circle of control. Those things that are within my circle of control I will disclose in my next and last chapter. Her safety and happiness are my mission. I will know when the time is right for her to be placed in a home. It is when she is no longer recognizing me or herself. Until then, she is stuck with me making her laugh, going for walks, watching her favorite Christmas specials and simply fulfilling my request I made in the parking lot some 25 odd years ago–"I just want to grow old with her", no matter what that looks like. That is my *Taste of Hope* currently. It has a flavor all its own.

CHAPTER 10

# LIFE LESSONS, OUTLOOKS, YOU DECIDE WHAT WORKS FOR YOU

I present you with this book as mentioned in the introduction. It is my outlook on experiences over the past 36 years or so. I have always had a struggle of whether I should write a book or not. I thought of doing it after Kevin was diagnosed. However, it didn't feel right. Then Brian's illness and then Marguerite's brain tumor. It was then I gave up on the thought. Certainly, there are times that we may reflect on what we have accomplished with our lives, be it a career, a business, a house, family etc. It was last year that I felt inspired.

Youth is a vibrant time to experience life. It feels like eternity is ahead of you. However, there were parts of my youth where I did not act as an adult. There were times of anger, rage, all due to my inability to deal with the life pressure I was feeling. I recall asking a father of a son who was older than Kevin what he does to relieve stress. He simply said a baseball bat and a tree. Beat that tree until you get all your anger out. I thought to myself, I could very well have a pile of sawdust by the time I'm done. I did not use that as pressure relief.

Yoga, I was told, was a good pressure relief. So, I took a night class at the local high schools. A month went by, and Kevin was still sick with Leukemia and I was still stressing. Yoga didn't work. My soul was seeking a cure for my son. It had nothing to do with Yoga and relieving stress.

I have exploded with anger at work, which a few times made people wonder what the hell was going on inside my head. Why is he snapping over something so trivial? People who are under deep stress from something that is very important to them are always near the potential breaking point. I often refer to it as the beach ball that is being held beneath the water. Deep and out of sight. Then something turns it loose and an emotion erupts that is as uncontrollable as stopping the beach ball once it has been released from its hold beneath the surface. Why does this happen? I think we are a society that does not plan for the painful unexpected. That would be identified as worrying and to most modern people would be considered a waste of time or dwelling on something that hasn't happened.

I recall going to a grocery store in Portland to pick up a couple of items and some balloons for Kevin while he was hospitalized. I saw a parking space open up, so as the car backed out, I placed my turn signal on. An elderly man pulled into the spot. My anger and hostility was out of control. I rolled the window down and screamed at him. He was completely innocent. He didn't do it out of spite, well at least I hope not. He saw an opportunity and took it. Maybe he just couldn't walk any further than was necessary to the entrance. I never considered that. My world was based on daily unplanned events. As a person who had a schedule, plans, agenda, goals, having a life with all unknowns and uncontrollable issues that arise at a moment's notice raises anxiety.

Living in a war-torn country is a comparison, however they are under a terrible kind of pressure that we cannot imagine. I have my deepest respect for those who have survived that trauma. I don't even think the old man heard me, but that action is not something I would do today. My point is this, people are neutral in behavior. We all have stimuli that comes into our days. Hopefully we are able to bear the bad with the good. However, when you see someone who is struggling, offer help, or simply be sympathetic and understanding. We don't know what is going on with someone's struggles that they keep hidden from the public eye. You can offer a kind word of, "You seem to need some help, what can I offer? I can listen, I can help with something on a physical level like loading groceries, but please, accept my offer and let me help."

There are several ideologies that expose themselves during times like this. There are the judgmental people who label this as Karma. Somehow bad fortune has entered a person's life because of something they did in their past. It is a way of thinking that everything comes full circle. Karma is a belief that I do not place value in, but respect those who believe in it. I'm sure there are situations where Karma is so applicable that it appears to be a mystical judge of justice and it will come after you based on your actions in the past. Okay, so if that is true, then let me say that based on the challenges

A Taste of Hope

in our lives, you'd think we drove tanks for Hitler and were receiving our payback.

There can be overlaps for anything if we look deep enough into it. I am now 60 years old, and it is a troubling age for me. I have a different perspective on life than most who find a complaint in some of the littlest issues. Yet there is an understanding that people struggle with minor problems because they lack exposure to solutions or are simply stuck behind roadblocks of issues and misfortune. I recall a parable that Eckhart Tolle spoke of. It was based on a story where a king wished for wisdom like the wiseman of his kingdom. In the end the king was presented with a ring that bore an inscription which he was prompted to read at any time he was troubled by difficulty. It read "This too will pass". Four words that reassure me that nothing lasts forever.

If you find that you are going through hard times you can't handle, there is a way out for you. Breathe and realize that tomorrow is another day. Do you recall that I mentioned both Marguerite and I had a tree picked out that we were going to drive into? Breathing and waiting for tomorrow is part of the answer. There are many songs out there that we can identify with. Some make us break down and cry immediately while others create the bravery in our souls to well up and provide us with courage. As I mentioned in an earlier chapter, the song by Phil Collins "In the Air Tonight" was something that I imagined putting a face to the invisible Leukemic cell that was trying to take Kevin's life. Like Marguerite's FTD we find it much easier to know who or what our enemy is. Maybe that is the reason we find ghosts so scary. We cannot see them and there is a thought that evil is attached to them. Otherwise, we would consider them angels. Demons, possessions, are also invisible things that have plagued mankind. I am not here to determine if they exist or are nothing but a myth that is carried over from one generation to the next.

It is true that we were brought onto this Earth with no instructions. Each parent does things in their unique way. We are products of our influences, and some become better from their negative world. We were in such parental pain when Kevin was going through chemotherapy. The clinic of Maine Children's Cancer program provided us with a video to watch. "When Bad Things Happen to Good People". It was first a book by a gentleman named Harold Kushner. It is in this that I realized that God is not capable of preventing evil from taking place. Kushner's outlook was to me, out of the box thinking. We as a culture not only in the west but globally look to God as the all-seeing judge and punisher for acts of wrongdoing. I believe that is a manmade concept. We have all seen it, and it is well depicted in movies.

We have a knack for begging God for favors and dreams. We pray that someone will be healed. Every generation, and especially in the 21$^{st}$ century where social media rules, we express ourselves with something that I feel is so shallow in meaning that we don't even realize we are doing it. Hugs and prayers are the words or memes often spread on social media. It is quick, it is heartfelt perhaps, but it dissolves as quickly as it was uttered.

I like to think that God has the ability to help by infusing someone's spirit to want to fight childhood cancer. Maybe to be a neurologist and actually saving someone's life and affecting so many others through their talents. There are fantastic people all over this planet who do jobs that others don't want to do. My hat is off to them, my appreciation for their skill in what they do.

Marguerite was given a two-hour pass to take Kevin out of the hospital once. She was 5 minutes away from the hospital when she got a flat tire. I was working and she was stranded on the side of the road in downtown Portland. At that moment she pulled over, stepped out of the vehicle to see the flat, and broke down and cried. She was broken. A two-hour break for her son to go to the mall, buy a toy, an ice cream, a little fun, was crushed.

It was then that a man driving through Portland with his wrecker truck pulled over to see why this woman was weeping on the side of the road. When she told him her predicament he sprang into action. Repaired the tire on sight, reinflated it and within 10 minutes she was road worthy. She pulled her check book out to pay him, and he merely said, "Have a nice day, enjoy your break with your son" and walked away refusing payment.

I never had the opportunity to thank him yet he has my deepest respect and admiration because he engaged his God given talent and wisdom to help someone in need. Perhaps some of you might be thinking that she could have changed her own tire, or that she should have had triple A? You were not in her shoes at that moment. That moment of feeling another defeat in trying to do something good for Kevin's spirit and happiness. This good Samaritan knew.

I have met some astounding people in my life. I have met some angry people in my life too. Perhaps some say the same of me, which is both understandable and okay. They are not wrong. Now I am not guilty of things that John Newton was before he wrote Amazing Grace, but I can honestly say that every day is a new beginning for all of us.

There are billions of people, perhaps trillions of people that have indeed faced far worse things than I. Horrific atrocities, and lifelong trials. I stand in the 21$^{st}$ Century on the shoulders of their failures as well as successes. This world is constantly changing, and people cannot seem to get along. We all see it, as some stopped watching the news. Some form an alliance with a specific type of group that shares their view. Their tribe is being cheated and they deserve to rise up and claim what is theirs. Think about it for a minute. It is rare that people find a way to get along anymore.

Now it is of the utmost importance that professional help is sought after. What type of professional help am I recommending? Counseling or seeing a professional psychologist or psychiatrist. In the beginning we started off slow and shallow by seeking out a councilor that we thought was putting us at ease. They are not a one size fits all. They have to be able to understand your personality, your needs, and most of all the pain that you are experiencing. They should also have a plan for you as to how progress looks and what goals to set for yourself based on your counseling. The psychiatry world is often viewed as something that weak people need because they cannot cope with reality. Based on poor upbringing? No life skills to know how to get them through the ordeal? It's a terrible stigma that is slowly fading and hopefully dies off sooner than later. Chiropractors too faced an uphill battle for respect of their field and in a lot of circles still do.

My wife's diagnosis of FTD (Frontotemporal Dementia) with the Aphasia variant actually put me in one of the deepest rabbit holes I could have experienced. Everything else that I experienced as a father and a husband I did so with my life long best friend by my side. We could share things and cry about things together because we knew each other on the deepest level. Her diagnosis was a relief because I knew what I was up against. But the hallucinations, the forgetfulness and the loss of her personality into the abyss of silence has been the most difficult. We are 4 years into this disease, and I am now feeling like I have a handle on it. I have gone through 3 counselors, and the caregivers that I had entrusted my wife with have been all over the spectrum. They have slept on the job, not been a good match, and disappeared from the world with no traceable forwarding address. All I wanted was someone to care for my wife while I go to work and support our lives.

Eckhart Tolle is an author who has several books about life and an understanding of its dynamics, based on how we interact with ourselves and the world around us. That description pales in comparison to what he has done for me. I have two audio books that I have listened to for the past 2 years, over and over while I make the 35-mile drive to work. That was a building block, but I still needed more help.

Out of my life experiences I knew with the state of mind I was in and facing what was ahead of me, I needed medication too. I found a group of both psychiatrists and counselors that help me both mentally and medicinally to face each day. I am not ashamed of what prescription drugs I take or who I see. In fact, it makes me strong to carry myself through the challenges of my day with balance and happiness. Even during the pandemic, facing my wife's needs and ever-changing developments, I am able to work with those that I try to keep safe as a safety manager at work.

There are adjustments that people have to make. Some hate change and any change that comes their way they fight against to some degree. Maybe a change at their job, a family member proclaiming news that affects them in some way, or perhaps it is the local or state government that is implementing something new that affects you. Through Eckhart Tolle's advice or teachings, I realize that there is nothing permanent on this planet. That includes me, my home, my family, or even in the long term, the planet itself. That is not a negative outlook but more along the lines of fact. Therefore as change occurs in my day, I make decisions that resolve an issue. As a safety professional I have to be a problem solver too. My daily life goes to problem solving both at work and home, at a moment's notice, and yes, some are planned as well.

The key to relaxing is to take microbreaks. I haven't really had a day off to myself and haven't had a vacation since 2019. But that is not to say that I need those things because I have adapted to enjoying the time when I do have microbreaks. Although I will say that writing this book has absorbed a lot of microbreak time, I am content with what I do for myself. Would I like more? Yes, who wouldn't regardless of what their current life status is? Ask anyone if they would like to have more vacation or relaxing time. Send up a flare when you find someone who says, "No thanks I'm good! In fact I was thinking of giving back some vacation time to my company I work for."

# A Taste of Hope

I daydream, and I try doing things on my own based on my solitude and loneliness. My work life is my social life. Primarily because my best friend depends on me to be there to care for her while at home. Combined with her excessive sleep patterns, traveling distances beyond 3 hours is difficult. She would do this for me in an instant. We have been through and succeeded in so many endeavors, it would kill us both for me to place her in a home. When I find myself staring out the window and feeling despair and grief, which Eminem depicts in lyrics of a duet song, as "window pane", I try to allow it some time, just allow it some time.

I think we all let out the thoughts which will haunt us if we do not allow them focal point time. Sounds silly? Think of a child rolling along in a carriage their mother is pushing. The child screams for minutes on end for something that would only fascinate his/her immediate need. That child's tantrum wanted attention therefore it seized the opportunity. Yes, I am comparing a child's action with negative thoughts of depression or despair. They are immediate occurrences. They stay until there is a distraction presented, then diminish sometimes as quickly as they arrived.

There are numerous additional comparisons, but I feel you have understood the point. My negative thinking comes from "My" brain. I am somehow generating it when I don't call for it. We all do this, I believe, depending on the situation. Maybe it's that big exam or the terrible reflection of how your current or past jobs made you feel terrible. Bury them and you have the beach ball underwater effect. Look at them as a message that your brain is trying to solve or resolve something. There are so many moments that I have forgotten, but a picture, an aroma, a dream brings it back to almost total recall. They were mostly great times, but the recall isn't there.

Then why do the bad memories pop up in our heads like it's a new TV commercial that is trying to get its airtime allotment over in a week instead of a month? I reflect on exactly why or what the problem is with these negative thoughts. Why this one? They occur within a 3 minute blip that may or may not continue. I let the thoughts play out. Fear? Anguish? Despair? Anger? Loneliness? All emotions that we are familiar with. Emotions that have invited themselves into our minds and influenced us down a dark road. Why is this memory coming up? I like to think that my brain is trying to understand it, feel right about it, because all those little neurons are communicating, telling the brain that this memory doesn't feel right.

What is it about this memory that needs addressing or solving? In a way this uninvited thought is like a child begging for their mother's attention by repeatedly saying, momma, momma, momma, momma etc. until momma answers her child with usually an abrupt "WHAT?" It's okay, we know who we are. This thought wants your attention. It won't stop, but it will keep coming back.

I want to sound like Smeagol in Lord of the Rings when he argues with his alter ego and says: "Leave, and never return!" But I believe it continues to come back until we resolve it or face it. This was part of my haunting through Kevin's leukemia, the terrible night terrors I had. Not many asked how I was doing. I was but Joseph, husband of Mary. The man who received little recognition in the Bible. I can count on one hand, over 36 years, those who would have the forethought and caring to ask, "How are you doing?"

Well would you look at that. I just shared with you another painful memory that has reared itself before me. But this one I have made peace with. I have grown to know and understand that no one means harm by not asking.

Less than 2% of 100 people have the capacity and ability to understand and work with quantum physics, so says the Google search I just performed. I am not in that percentage, as I have not been exposed to quantum physics and humbly, I would probably be lost with the first lesson. So how many people within that 100 have you been exposed to and have within your friend circle? The misunderstanding of the neighbor calling her children away because she didn't want them to catch leukemia. She didn't know what she didn't know. It was understandable. If she were a children's oncologist, I would view this differently. But nobody is as sinister as the villains or bad guys in the Hollywood movies.

The point is, when this memory comes back because it is still semi fresh in my mind, I do not become angry or enraged. I simply chalk it up to a situation in life that neither of us knew or had experience to handle. Did I always resolve issues like this? Absolutely not. I explained that I had night terrors through the years. I had to face my fears and pay attention to them. Resolve in my mind how to move on. Once I was able to do that, I was able to move on without those reoccurring and haunting memories.

I was fortunate to step into the world of Occupational Health & Safety where I had to think of how to prevent something from happening again. It was a foundation for problem solving for me. Then I started with an employer that infused problem solving for all aspects of the job. Knowing the simplest concepts of WHAT, WHY, and HOW is such a dynamic way of solving everyday problems let alone those issues of emotions and situations that you have no situational control over. What is the problem? Why is it a problem? How will I resolve this problem? That is all you need. Quantify what the problem is. If it doesn't actually present itself as one, then chalk it up to a problem resolved. If it does appear to be a problem, then dive down the rabbit hole to find out WHY? Make a list. Pick apart your problem. Your problem is now under attack. It is being analyzed and scrutinized for its legitimacy. Some of the issues that make it a problem will dissolve, while others will present themselves as low-hanging fruit. Easy for you to pick off and cast aside once you have resolved its minute contribution to the larger problem. Now suddenly, your problem is much smaller.

You have three things listed before you. (That is a figurative number). Is your problem starting to look like the playground bully who cries embarrassingly when punched in the nose because you were to be tired of it all? okay! It is not okay to allow yourself to be bullied. Stand up for yourself and those who mean something to you. No one else will.

Okay, two or three issues with this problem to resolve and it can be no longer feared? Sweet!! Let's do this!

Circle of control. There are things on this planet you have no control over. Sunrise, sunset, rain, snow, wind etc. Check the box if your contributing factor of a problem is well out of your control. What does that mean? It means that you accept it for what it is. An uncontrollable circumstance. But you will watch it like an eagle from up high who monitors the fields for the fleeting rabbit.

Now you are down to one or two. Even better. One of these contributing factors might be death. Feeling a life change after the death of a loved one? Who has failed to die on this planet? No one. I mean absolutely no one. Even Jesus died. So **Why** do I feel like death is the end? It is the worst outcome. Like the neighbor summoning her children, she doesn't know what she doesn't know. Neither do I, about life after death. So, respecting that variable, I realize that we are all going to leave this planet, spiritually at least. Do I have control over life? To some extent, yes. **What** can I do? Fill my presence with Love. Happiness. Non-worrying attitude. How is that perceived? A son sees his father unworried. He sees dad being happy and brave. Life must be good, or mom and dad would not be so happy. Same goes for my wife and her situations of a brain tumor and stroke and FTD. She needs to see my happiness and display of trust and strength.

This may sound a lot like an excerpt from the book Dianetics by L. Ron Hubbard. There is one specific concept which I agree with. But it takes modern medicine to contribute and solve the existing problem. If I were in danger, I would want to hear words of encouragement. We all know we are going to die someday, but if I were to have a disease that is going to take my life, I prefer to go out laughing and enjoying life with loved ones. Watching someone come in and hate being in the same room because they don't know what to say is unfair. Yes, the news is sad. So, are their final days not worth being happy? Stop moping and make their days filled with love, and sharing and memory making. Find strength within yourselves to fight and potentially be part of a miracle. Go for it. If it doesn't work, you and hopefully many like you went after what we all would want. Happiness. It isn't that easy, I understand. Wallowing in self pity can be part of the process, but for the sake of survival, find a way to climb out of it. I have climbed out of a few dark dismal moments and this book is to demonstrate that you too can do it, just keep trying. I have no super powers, nor was I born with a silver spoon of luxury and comfort above others.

Whatever it looks like. Baking and visiting while sharing coffee, treats, good times of laughter and joy. Continue it. Continue with ignoring the gloom of the loss and make it about them and not you. Remember the parable from Eckhart Tolle about the king who wanted what the wise man of the kingdom had. Wisdom. A ring inscribed: This too will pass. Be present, be part of that life like Mary was when Jesus hung on the cross before her. *The Taste of Hope* is the most amazing taste of all when you help someone face a difficult time.